A *Photographic* Guide to
BIRDS
OF AUSTRALIA

Peter Rowland
The Australian Museum

*Dedicated to my friend
and teacher, Walter.*

Published in Australia in 1999 by
New Holland Publishers (Australia) Pty Ltd
Sydney • Auckland • London • Cape Town
14 Aquatic Drive Frenchs Forest NSW 2086 Australia
218 Lake Road Northcote Auckland New Zealand
Garfield House 86 Edgware Road London W2 2EA United Kingdom
80 McKenzie Street Cape Town 8001 South Africa

First published in 1995
Reprinted in 1996, 1997, 1999, 2001, 2003, 2004

National Library of Australia Cataloguing-in-Publication Data

    Rowland, Peter, 1967-
    A photographic guide to birds of Australia
    Bibliography
    Includes index.
    Birds--Australia--Identification.
    Birds--Australia--Pictorial works.
    Also Titled: Birds of Australia

ISBN 1 85368 5992

Edited by Louise Egerton
Typeset by Anaconda Graphic Design
Reproduction by Hirt & Carter
Printed and bound by Times Offset (M) Sdn Bhd

Front cover: Australian King-Parrot (M. Prociv)
Back cover: Silvereye (G. Weber)
Spine: Laughing Kookaburra (P. German)
Title page: White-bellied Sea-Eagle (R. Brown)

Contents

Introduction

The function of this guide is to give the novice Australian birdwatcher the basic information necessary to identify the more commonly encountered species: concise texts and descriptive photographs are provided in a format that fits the pocket.

About 750 species of birds can be found in Australia. Many are migrants that appear only at certain times of the year; some are rare vagrants, with only a few sightings. Others have very limited distribution or live in areas that are difficult to access. Probably only a little more than half of the total are likely to be encountered on a regular basis by people who go to the easily-travelled parts of Australia. This book deals with these species.

With the aid of this guide, you will probably be able to identify most species that you encounter – or at least reduce the possibilities and place an unidentified bird in a particular family. You can then consult a more comprehensive book to make your identification.

Most Australian birds occur nowhere else. Some birdwatchers are driven to make confirmed sightings of as many as possible of these in a lifetime. Others are concerned to understand the biology and behaviour of birds and study relatively few in depth. This book has been written for the less motivated reader, who simply wants to identify a bird seen in a suburban garden or in the course of a walk through a national park. Be warned, however: birdwatching is addictive.

How to use this book

The text for each species account has been kept as concise as possible. Size (as total length and in some cases wingspan) is given beside the name of each species. Within the accounts, reference has been made to other species that may be confused with the species in question, or have such minute and obvious differences that they do not warrant an account of their own. Distribution maps show currently known ranges within Australia.

Classification of Australian birds

The classification of birds (like that of all animals) is an ongoing process, always subject to revision. Taking a reasonably modern view but avoiding major controversy, we can recognize 82 bird families in Australia. Several of these are of Australasian origin and either occur nowhere else or have their centre of distribution on the Australian subcontinent. Several families (e.g. ostriches and bulbuls) are exotic groups introduced to the subcontinent by Europeans.

ORDER STRUTHIONIFORMES

The Struthioniformes evolved on the ancient Gondwana supercontinent, and many species are still found in the southern hemisphere. All lack a keel on the sternum and all are flightless. Australia's native representatives are the Emu and Southern Cassowary (Casuariidae). The African Ostrich (Struthionidae) has been released from captive populations. All have strong legs, and have long loose (barbless) feathers. The body feathers of these species are double-shafted. All lack a hind toe, the Emu and Cassowary retaining three toes, the Ostrich simply two. Males undertake nesting duties away from their polygamous mates.

ORDER GALLIFORMES

Of the ground-frequenting specialists, the best known group includes the pheasants and quails. Their wings are rounded and they often have a large, heavy body and therefore have poor or limited flight. The beak is short and stout. Large feet, toes and claws are used to scratch for food on the ground, and strong legs contribute to rapid running. All have precocial young. Three families are represented in Australia. The mound builders (Megapodiidae) are large and best known for the construction, by males, of huge mounds of soil and fermenting vegetation in which the eggs are incubated. The true quails (Phasianidae) occupy open areas, and are usually gregarious. A third family (Odontophoridae) is represented by a single introduced species, the Californian Quail.

ORDER ANSERIFORMES

Members of this order have partially or fully webbed toes (with an associated swimming capability), a broad, flattened beak, and strong flight. The Magpie Goose (Anseranatidae) occurs only in Australia and New Guinea: it is long-legged, and has partially webbed toes. The swans and ducks (Anatidae) are short-legged, have fully webbed toes and are strong swimmers. They feed by grazing, dabbling at the water's edge or diving. All have precocial young.

ORDER PODICIPEDIFORMES

Grebes (Podicipedidae) are a cosmopolitan group of waterbirds. They are both swimmers and divers with legs placed well back on the body. The legs are laterally flattened and the toes are lobed (not webbed). The wings are reduced in size, restricting flight.

ORDER SPHENISCIFORMES

Penguins (Spheniscidae) are medium to large birds, with bold black and white plumage, confined to the southern hemisphere. Penguins swim well but cannot fly. The forelimbs are modified as flippers, with which the birds swim at speed both on and below the ocean surface.

ORDER PROCELLARIIFORMES

This order comprises the "true" seabirds, characterized by possession of long, thin wings adapted for continuous flight and webbed toes for swimming. It includes albatrosses, petrels, shearwaters and storm-petrels. Albatrosses (Diomedeidae) are the largest, their huge bodies having long plated beaks with basal nostril openings on the side of the bill. Smaller than these are the petrels and shearwaters (Procellariidae), in which the nasal cavities open at the top of the beak. Storm-petrels (Hydrobatidae) are the smallest and daintiest of the group, with longer and more delicate legs. Storm-petrels are similar to petrels in having the nasal opening on the top of the beak.

ORDER PELECANIFORMES

Members of this order have all four toes connected by webbing; all possess a throat-pouch (enormous in pelicans); and all have altricial young. Six families are represented in Australia. Tropicbirds (Phaethontidae) are pelagic by nature and gull-like in appearance: their distinguishing character is extremely long central tail feathers. Gannets and boobies (Sulidae) are oceanic, adapted to capture food by diving, often from great heights, into the sea. The Darter (Anhingidae) is remarkably like the cormorant, but differs in having a long, very thin neck, head and bill and a long tail; it also differs in behaviour. Cormorants (Phalacrocoracidae) are found in both salt and fresh water. Because the feathers lack the water-proofed capability of those of other aquatic birds, cormorants must spend time with their wings spread to dry. Food is captured underwater, the birds commencing the chase from a surface swimming position. Pelicans (Pelecanidae) are the largest members of the order: they have the longest beak and biggest throat pouch and, proportionately, the shortest legs. Food collection is done by dipping below the water surface. Frigatebirds (Fregatidae) are oceanic species possessing long thin wings, a strongly forked tail and heavily hooked bill. They take food from the surface and rob other species of their prey.

ORDER CICONIIFORMES
Herons and their allies are a group of long-legged, long-necked, wading birds. The young are all semi-altricial. Three families are represented in Australia. Herons (Ardeidae) have long legs and a long (often slender) beak. The neck has a spring-like action. In flight, the neck is normally held in a characteristic tight 'S' shape. Ibises and spoonbills (Threskiornithidae) have long legs and neck: the beak in the former is down-curved; in the latter, it is spatular. Ibisis and spoonbills fly with the head and neck outstretched. Storks (Ciconiidae) are long-legged, have a long stocky beak and fly with the neck outstretched.

ORDER FALCONIFORMES
Eagles, hawks and their kin are of cosmopolitan distribution. The beak is short, strongly hooked, and has a fleshy cere. The toes have sharp talons. Most are diurnal. The hawks and eagles (Accipitridae) generally possess rounded wings and fly relatively slowly. Falcons (Falconidae) have long, pointed wings and are fast fliers. They have a notched cutting edge on the maxilla.

ORDER GRUIFORMES
This diverse group is cosmopolitan: some possess, some lack, a hind toe. Cranes (Gruidae) are large and long-legged, with the hind toe raised above the others. Cranes are found in grassland and marsh. Rails (Rallidae) vary considerably in size: all have very slimly built bodies, and exhibit a hind toe. Many are aquatic and swim well; some are flightless. The plains-dwelling Bustard (Otididae) is bulkily built and spends most of its time on the ground, but is able to fly: it lacks a hind toe.

ORDER TURNICIFORMES
This small group comprises one family of button-quails (Turnicidae). These small, short-legged birds have a superficial resemblance to true quails but, among many differences, lack a hind toe and have many reversed sexual roles.

ORDER CHARADRIIFORMES
This large assemblage of varying sized wading, swimming and

flying birds contains many that are migratory. The young are either precocial or semi-precocial. There are ten Australian families, many with cosmopolitan affiliations. Uniquely Australian is the Plains Wanderer (Pedionomidae). Once thought to be allied to the button-quails, it is now recognized to be a wader. It has a hind toe and is sexually dimorphic: the male incubates the eggs and rears the chicks. Sandpipers, snipes and godwits (Scolopacidae) are common migrants, varying in size from diminutive to moderate. Most are cryptically coloured. Identification often depends on the relative lengths of beak and legs. All have unwebbed feet.

The Painted Snipe (Rostratulidae), which superficially resembles true snipes, is a cryptic species in which the male incubates the eggs and rears the chicks. Jacanas (Jacanidae) are rail-like and inhabit lily-covered lagoons and waterholes. Here their distinctive long toes allow them to walk across floating vegetation on the water's surface with ease. Stone-curlews or thick-knees (Burhinidae) are long-legged and nocturnal: they are accomplished runners, and often congregate in numbers during cooler months.

Oystercatchers (Haematopodidae) are moderately sized, with brightly coloured legs and colourful beaks: they haunt beaches and rocky headlands. Stilts and avocets (Recurvirostridae) are delicate, long-legged birds with beaks that are, respectively, needle-thin and straight; or thin and upcurved. Moderate to small sized waders are the widespread plovers, dotterels and lapwings (Charadriidae). These have a short beak, round head and short neck. They are often gregarious.

Pratincoles (Glareolidae) possess long streamlined wings and a short tail. One species has short legs, in the other they are long and thin. Pratincoles feed from the ground and on the wing. Terns and gulls (Laridae) are characterized by having webbed toes on short legs, and long pointed wings. They are gregarious, swim and obtain food from the surface of the water by diving (terns) or by scavenging (gulls).

ORDER COLUMBIFORMES

This order is cosmopolitan but only one family (Columbidae) is represented in Australia. Pigeons are both terrestrial and arboreal. Many species exhibit brilliantly coloured plumage, either completely or as iridescent patches. All construct a fragile nest and lay white eggs. The young are altricial and are fed on a liquid 'pigeon milk' produced by the parent.

ORDER PSITTACIFORMES

Parrots are easily recognized by their bright colours; short, hooked beak; and a foot with two toes directed forward and two to the rear. All parrots use the beak in climbing. Two families of parrots are readily distinguished: the cockatoos (Cacatuidae), and the lorikeets and typical parrots (Psittacidae). The former are large crested parrots restricted in distribution to Australia and the south-west Pacific. The remaining parrots may have brush-like tongues (lorikeets) or typical thick, horny tongues. Most are gregarious and noisy. A number have fleshy ceres, or colourful areas of bare skin.

ORDER CUCULIFORMES

Most Australian cuckoos are nest parasites, laying eggs in the nests of other birds, which incubate and feed the intruders. All cuckoos have slightly decurved beaks and short legs; two toes point forward and two back. Two families occur in Australia: the typical nest-usurping cuckoos (Cuculidae) and the nest-constructing and parentally inclined coucal (Centropodidae).

ORDER STRIGIFORMES
Like the diurnal raptors, many nocturnal owls possess strong legs and talons. They differ from Falconiformes in the structuring of the feathers that ensure silent flight and the feet, which have two toes directed forward and two to the rear. Their eyes are directed forward and are adapted for nocturnal vision. Hawk owls (Strigidae) have rounded heads and short legs. Barn owls (Tytonidae) have large facial disks and long legs. Both families vary from moderately sized to large birds.

ORDER CAPRIMULGIFORMES
Nightjars, owlet-nightjars and frogmouths are nocturnal. They lack the talons and associated actions of the Strigiformes, and most have frail legs. They hunt by pouncing on prey and swallowing it whole. Three families occur in Australia. The largest birds are the frogmouths (Podargidae), characterized by their size, wide beaks and choice of retiring to rest on a branch of a tree. The nightjars (Caprimulgidae) are long-winged and feed by aerial pursuit. Their feet are weak, and they possess large eyes and are ground-nesters. One owlet-nightjar (Aegothelidae) occurs in Australia. It is small, has a wide beak, soft plumage and big bulbous eyes. It nests and roosts in hollow limbs.

ORDER APODIFORMES
Swifts and swiftlets are long-winged and extremely weak-legged. There is one family in Australia (Apodidae). The tail of the two larger species is spiny. They are aerial feeders capturing flying prey in the short, very wide, beak. Saliva is used in their nest construction, which is undertaken in caves and crevices.

ORDER CORACIIFORMES
Kingfishers, bee-eaters and rollers are brightly coloured birds, all with weak legs and syndactyl toes. Members of the four Australian families have a large head and a heavy beak. The water-kingfishers (Alcedinidae) nest in hollows along waterways and feed principally by diving into water. The terrestrial kingfishers (Halcyonidae) nest in hollow trees and earthen banks and characteristically feed by securing prey from trees or the ground. The long-winged bee-eaters (Meropidae) have long central tail feathers. The slender and slightly decurved beak is employed in aerial feeding. The single Australian species nests in an earthen burrow. Rollers (Coraciidae) have long, pointed wings and a short but wide beak. They are aerial feeders and nest in tree hollows.

ORDER PASSERIFORMES
Song- or perching birds make up the remaining (34) families of Australian birds belonging in one immense order. Anatomically, they all display a distinctive palate and have three toes forward and one to the rear. The young are altricial. Gaudily coloured pittas (Pittidae) are very distinctive. They have short, rounded wings,

long legs, and are generally terrestrial. Lyrebirds (Menuridae) and scrub-birds (Atrichornithidae) are also largely terrestrial: both have short, rounded wings. Lyrebirds have stout legs and feet. A long tail on the male is used in elaborate displays. The closely related scrub-birds are known for their loud, ringing song and proficient mimickry. They are cryptic and elusive birds, secreting themselves in dense understorey.

Treecreepers (Climacteridae) have a long, decurved beak and feed principally from limbs and trunks of trees. Fairy-wrens (Maluridae) are small birds and, generally, adult males are the brightest coloured. Both sexes have a short, weak beak, a long tail and short and rounded wings. Pardalotes (Pardalotidae) differ in being arboreal, choosing to nest in hollows of trees or those evacuated in the soil. Also included in the family is a number of small species commonly called 'little brown birds': gerygones, thornbills and scrubwrens, which can be terrestrial or arboreal. All have thin beaks and short, weak, rounded wings.

A large songbird family, the honeyeaters (Meliphagidae), is characteristic of Australia; nearly all species have slender, decurved beaks. Related to honeyeaters are the Australian chats, which are mainly ground-haunting. In all species the tongue is bifurcate and brush-tipped, the wings short and rounded. Another family of Australasian origin comprises the robins (Petroicidae). These are best characterized by their small size, often colourful plumage, rictal bristles, short, weak legs and beaks. Logrunners (Orthonychidae) are also a group of ancient Australian origin. They are terrestrial and have short, rounded wings and long, stout legs.

Babblers (Pomatostomidae) are gregarious, have a long, strong and decurved beak, short and rounded wings, and short and stout legs. Quail-thrushes and whipbirds (Cinclosomatidae) are typically ground-dwelling. Some have a long, pointed beak; all have stout legs and rounded wings. Among the arboreal groups are the minute sittellas (Neosittidae) with a beak that is thin, short and gently upcurved. They climb and feed from limbs and trunks of trees.

Superficially resembling the robins (but larger) are the whistlers and shrike-thrushes (Pachycephalidae). These have a rounded head, a stout, hooked beak and short, pointed wings. Another flycatching group includes the fantails, Magpie-lark and drongos (Dicruridae). These have a broad head; a long, hooked, but sometimes weak, bill; long wings; and short legs. All possess rictal bristles. The Magpie-lark is the only member of this family to construct a nest of mud. Cuckoo-shrikes (Campephagidae) have a stout beak, which is slightly decurved. The nostrils are partly hidden by short bristles. The wings are pointed and the legs short and weak.

Orioles (Oriolidae) are widespread through Africa to Asia and Australia. Two genera occur in Australia, the Figbird being restricted to Australia, New Guinea and eastern Indonesia. All orioles have a long bill and long, pointed wings. The legs are short and stout. Figbirds are similar to orioles but have a broader bill. Woodswallows, butcherbirds, magpies and currawongs are now placed in the same family (Artamidae). Woodswallows are typical aerial feeders, spending much time on long, pointed wings. The tail and legs are stout, the bill is short and stout, and the tongue is brush-tipped. Butcherbirds, magpies and currawongs all have stout, hooked beaks. Bright iridescent colours dominate in male birds-of-paradise (Paradisaeidae).

Within the bowerbirds and catbirds (Ptilonorhynchidae) the brightly coloured males construct bowers of sticks, which may be decorated by coloured ornaments. Crows and ravens (Corvidae) are large birds, with black iridescent feathering. Their legs are stout and they have long, feathered rictal bristles. Mud-nesting is a characteristic of a very small family (Corcoracidae): both species are gregarious and terrestrial. Larks (Alaudidae) possess pointed wings, a long hind claw and a distinctive display flight. Pipits and wagtails (Motacillidae) are terrestrial and have long pointed wings, a beak that is thin and pointed, and an elongated hind toe.

An introduction of sparrows (Passeridae) in the 19th century has caused these birds to be well-distributed throughout eastern Australia. Their short, conical beak and short legs are very distinctive. The native grass finches are related. Several species of true finches (Fringillidae) have been introduced from Europe: these have rounded wings, a short, conical bill and short legs. Sunbirds (Nectariniidae) are represented by one small but brightly coloured species with a long decurved beak and partly tubular tongue. Another family with only one Australian representative comprises the flowerpeckers (Dicaeidae). Typically, these have short legs and short and pointed beaks but the wings of the Australian species are long and pointed.

Swallows and martins (Hirundinidae) are aerial-feeding species with long pointed wings and weak legs. The beak is short and wide, bordered by rictal bristles. Bulbuls (Pycnonotidae) are exotic birds introduced by Europeans. They possess rictal bristles and short wings, the legs are short and weak. Smaller-sized birds with remarkably melodious songs include the cosmopolitan old-world warblers (Sylviidae) which have a slender beak, and wings that are short and usually rounded. Silvereyes or white-eyes (Zosteropidae) are widespread from Africa, Asia and the south Pacific islands to Australia. Apart from a ring of white feathering about the eyes, these small birds are generally grey or yellow in colour. They have straight, slender bills. The legs are short, and the wings are rounded.

Australian species of thrushes and thrush-like birds (Muscicapidae) are generally terrestrial in habit. They have long slender beaks, the legs are stout, and the wings rounded or pointed. Introductions from Europe and Asia are the gregarious Common Myna and Common Starling (Sturnidae). They, and the native species, have straight, pointed bills and strong legs.

Bird habitats and distribution

Australia comprises a wide variety of environments, ranging from the tropical rainforests of northern Queensland to the alpine scrubs of Mount Kosciusko. This has encouraged the evolution of a rich diversity of birds.

Grassland is the most extensive environment, followed by scrubland and woodland, then dry and wet eucalypt forests. There are relatively small areas of rainforest, wetlands, heathland, coastal mudflats and mangroves.

The habitats of most birds are restricted to one or a few of these environments – usually to particular components of them. Most environments are shared by a number of species that exploit different resources of food and shelter. Many species may appear to share the same habitat but close examination usually reveals that they are separated by behaviour: one may feed on the ground, another in mid-level vegetation, another in the tree canopy. Some species are sedentary, spending their entire lives in one area. Others move nomadically between similar habitats in response to the availability of food, or migrate very great distances

– sometimes from one hemisphere to the other. As a general rule, better watered environments are home to a greater number of sedentary species than those with lower or less regular rainfall. Arid grasslands have the lowest proportion of resident species.

Whether sedentary or mobile, every species has habitat requirements that are limited by available environments. It is self-evident that if the extent of a particular environment (such as tropical rainforest or temperate wetland) is diminished, certain habitats will decrease, leading to reduction in the population of birds that depend upon these habitats – a process that can lead to extinction. It is equally self-evident that agriculture, forestry and urbanization have led – and continue to lead – to destruction of most natural environments, except where areas have been set aside as national parks or similar reserves. Rather surprisingly, no mainland bird species has yet become extinct but a number are very vulnerable and may not persist long into the 21st century.

Bird biology

Parts of a bird

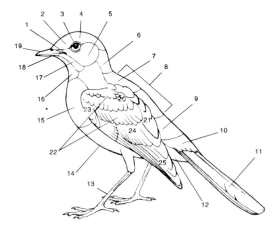

1 lores	10 uppertail coverts	19 upper mandible
2 forehead	11 tail	20 scapulars
3 eye-ring	12 undertail coverts	21 tertials
4 crown	13 tarsus	22 wing coverts
5 ear coverts	14 belly	23 alula
6 nape	15 breast	24 secondaries
7 mantle	16 throat	25 primaries
8 back	17 malar region	
9 rump	18 lower mandible	

Emu *Dromaius novaehollandiae* Up to 2m

R.W.G. Jenkins

This bird's grey-brown body feathers consist of two long plumes which are attached at the base of each black feather shaft. The male and female have similar plumage. The black upper-neck feathers are thinly scattered and allow the blue skin to show through, this is slightly darker in female birds. Emus pair for about five months of the year and egg-laying commences in April or May. The 7 to 20 dark green eggs are hatched solely by the male. Found in all but the densest forests and most heavily populated areas, this large, flightless bird is a common sight over much of Australia.

Southern Cassowary *Casuarius casuarius* 1.5-2m

Dick Whitford

The prominent greyish casque and red wattle hanging from the neck, make the Southern Cassowary easily identifiable. The feathers of the body are black and hair-like, becoming more rufous toward the tail. The bare skin of the head and fore-neck is blue, while the hind-neck is red. The female is generally taller than the male and has a taller casque. Calls consist of a variety of guttural rumblings and grunts. Uncommon and wary. Attacks on humans have been recorded, especially during the breeding season, June to October. The elusive Southern Cassowary inhabits the dense rainforests of northern Queensland.

Hoary-headed Grebe *Poliocephalus poliocephalus* 27-30cm

The upperparts of the Hoary-headed Grebe are generally grey and underparts are white. During the breeding season the throat turns black and the head becomes dark grey with numerous overlying white plumes. The male is slightly larger than the female and has a pale golden-yellow eye, speckled with black. When observed in the field, a bird seldom allows close approach and generally flies off at the sight of an intruder. Prey consists mainly of aquatic insects and crustaceans, caught in underwater dives. Probably the most gregarious of the grebe family, it is often seen nesting and roosting in groups on unsheltered areas of fresh and brackish waterways.

R. Drummond

Australasian Grebe *Tachybaptus novaehollandiae* 25-27cm

G. Little

Outside of the breeding season, this species is often confused with the **Hoary-headed Grebe** but can be distinguished by its yellow eye. During the breeding season, September to March, both sexes attain a rich chestnut facial stripe that extends from just behind the eye through to the base of the neck. The remainder of the head becomes glossy black and the oval patch of bare skin at the base of the bill becomes pale yellow. Food, which consists mainly of small fish and water insects, is normally caught during deep underwater dives but some prey is taken on the surface.

Great Crested Grebe *Podiceps cristatus* 46-50cm (Females smaller than males)

P. Slater

When in breeding plumage, November to February, this large grebe is resplendent with its beautiful chestnut and black tippets and glossy black crest. Outside of the breeding season it has a black crown with a reduced crest, dark brown upperparts and white underparts, tinged with rufous on the flanks. During the breeding season both sexes perform an elaborate mating display, in which both birds face each other and rear up on their tails, becoming almost vertical out of the water. Found on extensive, open waterways, it feeds on a wide variety of aquatic animals and plants.

Little Penguin *Eudyptula minor* 32-34cm

R.L. Smith

The smallest of the penguins found in Australian waters and the only species to breed on the Australian mainland. At rest, the bird lies on the surface of the water with its flippers outstretched. The underparts, including the underside of the flippers, are white and the upperparts are dark blue, camouflaging it against the surrounding water. The eye is silver-grey and the bill is black. Food, which consists of fish and squid, is caught by skilful underwater pursuits. Unlike other penguins, it waits for the cover of night before coming ashore to roost. It occurs throughout southern Australia.

14

Wandering Albatross *Diomedea exulans* 80-135cm; Wingspan 260-325cm

G. Robertson

Often seen scavenging from fishing boats, the Wandering Albatross appears entirely white at a distance. Closer inspection reveals fine black wavy lines on the breast neck and upper back. The white tail is occasionally tipped with black and the back of the wings change from black to white with age. The female is slightly smaller than the male and has brown speckles on the crown. The Wandering Albatross spends most of the year roaming the southern parts of the globe in an effortless glide, resting occasionally on the water's surface to feed on squid, fish and waste from boats. It occurs in Australian waters between June and September.

Black-browed Albatross *Diomedea melanophris* 85-88cm; Wingspan 220-240cm

G.W. Johnstone

The slate-black back and upper wing of the Black-browed Albatross is very striking against the contrasting white of its head, neck and underparts. This, combined with the bird's 'smudged' grey-black eyebrow, makes it instantly recognizable. The bill is yellow-orange, becoming more red at tip, and the feet are grey-blue. Sub-adult birds have more black on

the underwing. For most of the year this is the most commonly seen albatross off the southern Australian coastline. Although recorded in Australian waters in all months of the year it is most common between May and October, arriving a few weeks ahead of the **Wandering Albatross**.

15

Southern Giant-Petrel *Macronectes giganteus* 85-90cm; Wingspan 200-220cm

C. Gill

The distinctive tube-nosed bill, which is rather pale and finishes in a pale green bulbous tip, distinguishes this bird from the **Northern Giant-Petrel**, which has a dark pink-brown tip. The most common colour for birds found in Australia is dark brown, adults having a white head and upper neck. The white form of this species is mostly confined to areas around the Antarctic Circle. Superficially resembling an albatross in size and shape, the immature Southern Giant-Petrel is a regular visitor to coastal areas of southern Australia. Common in offshore areas and harbours.

White-headed Petrel *Pterodroma lessonii* 40-46cm (Females smaller than males)

T. Palliser

The white head, breast and belly, with contrasting mottled grey-black upperparts and black wings, distinguish this bird from other petrels found in Australian waters. Spending much of its time at sea, it feeds at night on squid and fish, plucked from the surface of the water. The White-headed Petrel is mainly solitary, pairing only for the breeding season, August to May. Although birds are usually silent when at sea, breeding colonies are quite noisy, uttering a variety of high-pitched 'wik-wik-wik' and braying 'oooo-er' calls. It occurs off the southern Australian coastline in late summer and winter.

Great-winged Petrel *Pterodroma macroptera* 40-42cm

N. Kolichis

This uniformly blackish-brown petrel is easily identified by its large size and absence of pale markings on the body. Normally solitary, it pairs only for the breeding season, from January to October. Outside the breeding season it spends its time at sea, hunting by night for krill and squid, which it scoops from the surface of the water. It is usually silent at sea but breeding colonies are noisy places, with a variety of staccato 'kik-kik-kik' or 'si-si-si' calls being uttered in the air and at the nest. It is common on offshore islands and open ocean off the southern Australian coast.

Fairy Prion *Pachyptila turtur* 23-25cm

M. Carter

With the exception of the **Fulmar Prion**, which is not found in Australian waters, the Fairy Prion is the 'bluest' of its family. Chiefly blue-grey above and white below, it can also be distinguished from other prions by its short dark blue bill. It has a robust hook on the tip of the upper mandible, leaving only a short space between it and the nasal tubes. A dark black 'M' is visible on the back of the wings when in flight. The Fairy Prion is the only prion to breed in Australia. It is common in offshore and coastal areas of southern Australia.

Wedge-tailed Shearwater *Puffinus pacificus* 42-47cm

T. Lindsey

The diagnostic long, wedge-shaped tail clearly distinguishes this species from other shearwaters. After moult, the plumage is a dark glossy black but soon turns to the usual dark brown with wear. The Wedge-tailed Shearwater has a less common pale morph, in which the underparts are white, as are the centres of the underwings. The upperparts are pale brown with a faint 'M' visible on the wings and back, when in flight. Immatures resemble adults in both forms. The Wedge-tailed Shearwater usually occurs alone or in small groups. It is found on both the eastern and western coastlines of Australia.

Short-tailed Shearwater *Puffinus tenuirostris* 40-43cm

J.R. Napier

The Short-tailed Shearwater is dark brown in plumage, the underwing occasionally having traces of white in the centre. The tail is rounded and, when in flight, the dark grey feet trail slightly behind. This species should not be confused with the **Sooty Shearwater**, which is larger with a longer bill. Immature birds are similar in plumage to the adults. During summer, this is the most common shearwater along the south and south-eastern coasts of Australia: at this time many dead and dying birds may be found washed up on beaches.

Wilson's Storm-Petrel *Oceanites oceanicus* 15-19cm

P. Morris/Ardea

This sooty black bird, with a square tail and white rump, does not resemble any other storm-petrel found off the Australian coast. The underside of its feet are yellow and, in flight, protrude beyond the end of the tail. When feeding, its flight resembles that of a butterfly, wings held high, bouncing erratically above the surface of the water as it collects whale oil and blubber and small crustaceans. It is the most common storm-petrel found on Australia's continental shelf, particularly along the east and west coasts.

White-faced Storm-Petrel *Pelagodroma marina* 18-20cm

G. Robertson

As its name suggests, this species is easily distinguished by its conspicuous white face pattern. The upperparts are almost entirely dark grey, with a paler grey rump; underparts are white. It feeds on krill and small squids, taken from the surface of the water. Breeding takes place in small colonies on offshore islands, between September and April. The White-faced Storm-Petrel is the most common storm-petrel found in Australian waters, occasionally sighted off Tasmania and the coastline of mainland south-eastern Australia.

Australian Pelican *Pelecanus conspicillatus* 160-180cm

D. & M. Trounson

With its enormous pouched bill and bulky frame, the pelican is unmistakable when fishing or at rest on land. The female is slightly smaller than the male, but both share the characteristic black and white plumage. Immature birds are brown where adults are black. When soaring high (up to 3000m) on thermal currents, it is often confused with the **White-bellied Sea-Eagle**. Breeding is opportunistic, and commences when there is sufficient rain or available ground water. Pelicans are found on rivers, lakes and coastal mudflats throughout all but the most arid areas of Australia.

Australasian Gannet *Morus serrator* 84-95cm

J.R. Napier

The male and female are similar in plumage: most of the body is white with darkened tips to the major wing feathers and the inner tail feathers. The head is buff-yellow and the bill is pale blue-grey with striking black borders to the bill sheaths. In immature birds the head and upperparts are mostly brown with inconsistent amounts of white spotting. Familiar off the southern coast of Australia, the Australasian Gannet forms small flocks that soar ten or more metres above the surface of the water, then fold their wings back and dive into the water in pursuit of fish.

Darter *Anhinga melanogaster* 85-90cm

B. Chudleigh

Male Darters are predominantly glossy black with buff-cream streaks on the upper wing. The bill is yellow and sharply pointed, and a white stripe extends from below the eye to the first curve of the neck. Females are light grey brown where the males are black and the white eye-stripe is bordered with black. Young birds resemble the female in plumage but lack the eye-stripe. Sitting quietly in the water with its body submerged and only its head and neck visible, the Darter will sink silently under water to pursue fish, insects and small turtles for up to a minute at a time.

Little Pied Cormorant *Phalacrocorax melanoleucos* 50-60cm

G. Little

The Little Pied Cormorant is entirely black above and white below. The face is dusky and, in adult birds, the white of the underside extends above the eye. It is easily distinguished from the larger **Pied Cormorant**, which has an orange-yellow face patch. One of the more common Australian waterbirds, the Little Pied Cormorant is at home on virtually any body of water, fresh or saline, throughout Australia. It is often seen in large flocks on open waterways and on the coast, especially where large numbers of fish are present. On inland streams and dams, however, it is often solitary.

Great Cormorant *Phalacrocorax carbo* 70-90cm

G. Little

This is the largest of the Australian cormorants and one of the largest in the world. It is almost entirely black in plumage, apart from a small white patch on each thigh (absent in winter), and can be distinguished from the **Little Black Cormorant** by its larger size and by the white chin and yellow throat. In spite of its preference for extensive areas of permanent fresh water, the Great Cormorant is by no means confined to these and is often observed on coastal inlets and estuaries. It occurs throughout most of Australia but is more numerous in the south-east and south-west.

Little Black Cormorant *Phalacrocorax sulcirostris* 60-65cm

M. Carter

This common cormorant is easily distinguished from the **Great Cormorant** by its entirely black plumage, including the face and bill, and its smaller size. The feathers of the back have a faint green gloss, which is not always visible. Where food is abundant it often forms large flocks. It is a familiar sight on farm dams and small ponds (often in the company of the **Little Pied Cormorant**) and is a regular visitor to the flood waters of the interior. Its preference for fresh water, especially small lakes and ponds, and its tolerance of salt water environments make it a common sight throughout most of Australia.

White-necked Heron *Ardea pacifica* 76-105cm

Hans & Judy Beste

Its large size and distinct white head and neck, with a double row of brown-black spots on the front, distinguish the White-necked Heron from any other Australian heron or egret. The lower breast and belly are grey-brown, streaked with white, while the back and wings are chiefly grey-black (with long maroon plumes on the back in the breeding season). In flight, a conspicuous white patch is visible on the bend (elbow) of each wing. It is largely nomadic, favouring wet grasslands, freshwater wetlands and, less commonly, coastal waters over much of Australia. It is common throughout its range.

White-faced Heron *Egretta novaehollandiae* 60-70cm

G. Hoye

The most familiar heron in Australia, it is easily identified by its primarily blue-grey plumage and a characteristic white face. When disturbed it rises to the air in a slow bouncing flight with its long neck outstretched, croaking in alarm as it goes. In flight the darker flight feathers are contrasted against the paler grey plumage, making it easily identifiable when viewed from below. This species feeds on a wide variety of prey, including fish, insects and amphibians. It is found on any suitable body of water throughout the mainland and Tasmania, from tidal mudflats to moist grasslands.

Cattle Egret *Ardea ibis* 48-53cm

K. Ireland

Smallest of the Australian egrets, this bird should not be confused with the larger **Intermediate Egret**, which occasionally occupies similar habitat. Both species have a yellow bill (unlike the **Little Egret**, which has a predominantly black bill). The Cattle Egret walks with a very obvious back-and-forth head movement. For most of the year it has almost entirely white plumage but, during the breeding season (October to January), it is distinguished by long, dark golden plumes on the head, neck, breast and mantle. It is commonly seen in small flocks, opportunistically feeding on grasshoppers, and other insects, that are disturbed by grazing cattle.

Great Egret *Ardea alba* 41-49cm

G. Weber

This is the largest of the Australian egrets. The plumage is white and, for most of the year, the bill and facial skin are yellow. During the breeding season (October to December) long nuptial plumes hang from the mantle and at this time the bill is mostly black and the facial skin is green. The length of its neck is greater than the length of its body. The Great Egret usually feeds alone but roosts at night in groups and breeds in colonies, usually in association with cormorants and ibises, as well as other egrets. Common throughout most of Australia, and indeed the world.

Nankeen Night Heron *Nycticorax caledonicus* 55-65cm

L.F. Schick

Quite distinct from other herons in Australia, the Nankeen Night Heron has rich cinnamon-rufous upperparts and a black crown. Three long white plumes which cascade from the back of the head are retained throughout the year, unlike some other herons. Young birds are often confused with bitterns, especially the **Australasian Bittern**, due to their streaked plumage. However, the narrower streaking of the heron's underparts and the regular 'tear-drop' spotting on its wings and back should distinguish it in the field. It frequents shallow, sheltered waterways and flooded grasslands where it feeds on fish, aquatic insects, small crustaceans and amphibians. It is nocturnal.

Black-necked Stork *Ephippiorhynchus asiaticus* 129-137cm

C. Andrew Henley/Larus

The only member of the stork family found in Australia. The black and white body plumage, glossy dark green and purple neck and massive black bill distinguish this bird from all other Australian birds. The female has yellow eyes. In flight, the long coral-red legs trail behind the body and the long neck and bill are held outstretched. Immature birds resemble adults, but the black plumage is brown and the white plumage is more grey-brown. Mostly restricted to coastal and near-coastal areas of northern and eastern Australia, it feeds on fish, small crustaceans and amphibians in lagoons, swamps and tidal mudflats.

Australian White Ibis *Threskiornis molucca* 69-76cm

D. & M. Trounson

The Australian White Ibis is identified by almost entirely white body plumage and black head and neck. The head is featherless and its black bill is long and down-curved. During the breeding season the small patch of skin on the under-surface of the wing changes from dull pink to dark scarlet. Adult birds have a tuft of cream plumes on the base of the neck. Frequenting swamps, lagoons and floodplains, as well as urban parks and gardens, it feeds on a wide variety of foods, from aquatic insects and crustaceans to human refuse. Well adapted to all but the most arid habitats, it is common and widespread.

Straw-necked Ibis *Threskiornis spinicollis* 59-76cm

T. Newbery

The commonest and most striking of the Australian ibises, this species is identified by its iridescent purple-green back and wings and snow-white underparts. The down-curved bill is black, as is the bare skin of the head and neck; the lower neck is covered with short feathers. Long 'straw-like' plumes cascade from the fore-neck (these are absent on young birds). During the breeding season the bare yellow skin of the under-wing becomes bright red. It often occurs in large flocks in wet or dry grasslands over much of Australia, feeding on terrestrial invertebrates.

Glossy Ibis *Plegadis falcinellus* 48-61cm

D. & M. Trounson

This is the smallest ibis found in Australia and has an unmistakable colouration. It is entirely dark chestnut with an iridescent purple and green sheen, darker green on the wings. When not breeding the head is dull brown with some white streaking. The male has a slightly longer bill than the female. Mostly inhabiting shallow freshwater lagoons and flooded pastures, it is also found in mangroves and on estuarine mudflats, feeding on insects, fish and crustaceans. The Glossy Ibis is very nomadic, foraging in groups, often quite large ones, and over a wide area. It occurs over much of the Australian mainland.

Royal Spoonbill *Platalea regia* 75-80cm

D. & M. Trounson

The Royal Spoonbill is easily identified by its white plumage and black spatulate bill (in contrast to the pale yellow bill of the **Yellow-billed Spoonbill**). The Royal Spoonbill feeds in shallow lagoons and swamps, catching small fish and crustaceans by sweeping its head from side to side. During the breeding season long white plumes descend from the nape; these are lacking in young birds. It usually occurs alone or in small groups but breeds in colonies which can be quite large. It is almost silent. Of the two Australian spoonbills, the Royal Spoonbill is the more common and is found extensively throughout the northern and eastern parts of Australia.

Magpie Goose *Anseranas semipalmata* 71-92cm (Females smaller than males)

C. Andrew Henley/Larus

This large, noisy goose is readily recognized. The head and neck are black and there is a characteristic knobbed crown. The underparts are white, with contrasting black margins on the underwing. The legs, feet and bill are orange. It frequents floodplains and wet grasslands from Fitzroy River, Western Australia, through northern Australia to Rockhampton, Queensland, and occasionally south to the Hunter River,

New South Wales. The Magpie Goose is a specialised feeder, with wild rice *Oryza*, *Panicum*, *Paspalum* and spike-rush *Eleocharis* forming the bulk of its diet. It is gregarious, often forming vast, noisy flocks.

Black Swan *Cygnus atratus* 120-142cm (Females smaller than males)

Dick Whitford

This is the only black swan found anywhere in the world. In flight the neck is held outstretched and the broad white wing tips contrast against the otherwise black body. The bill is a deep orange-red with a distinct narrow white band and paler white nail at the tip of the upper mandible. Introduced into several countries and a vagrant to New Guinea, the Black Swan favours extensive waterways and permanent wetlands where it feeds mainly on algae. It can be observed throughout Australia, with the exception of Cape York Peninsula, but is more common in the south.

Plumed Whistling-Duck *Dendrocygna eytoni* 44-62cm

K. Ireland

The Plumed Whistling-Duck is paler than its close relative the **Wandering Whistling-Duck**. Mostly brown above, paler yellow-brown on head and neck, and pale brown below, it has a rufous breast, conspicuously barred with black. The long flank plumes are cream with black margins. In flight, its speckled underwing, white belly and pink legs make it easily identifiable. Rarely observed in the water, it feeds on grasses, herbs and sedges on the margins of swamps and lagoons or open pastures often far from water. It is found in dense flocks throughout much of eastern and northern Australia.

Pacific Black Duck *Anas superciliosa* 50-60cm

Dick Whitford

The dark brown line through the eye, bordered with cream above and below, and a dark brown crown make this duck easily distinguishable at a distance. The upper body feathers are mid-brown, each feather being edged with buff, and the underparts are mottled brown. Upperwing colour is the same as the back, with a bright green sheen on the secondaries. The white underwing is conspicuous in flight. One of the most versatile of the Australian ducks, it frequents all types of water, from isolated forest pools to tidal mudflats. It is found in all but the most arid regions of Australia.

Grey Teal *Anas gracilis* 40-48cm

D. Hadden

At rest, this duck is easily overlooked. It is almost entirely grey-brown, each feather of the body being edged with buff, except on the rump. The chin and throat are white, (distinguishing it from the female **Chestnut Teal**, which has a pale brown chin and throat). The eye is red and the bill is dark blue-grey. The secondary wing feathers are glossy black (with a blue sheen) above, tipped with white, and have broad white bases. In flight these white bases form a horizontal white stripe which becomes wider towards the body. It is common in all sheltered aquatic habitats throughout Australia.

Chestnut Teal *Anas castanea* 38-48cm

L. Robinson

The endemic Chestnut Teal is most common throughout the southern parts of its range. The male is easily identified by its green head, dappled chestnut breast and belly, brown back and diagnostic white flank patch. The female is quite drab in comparison, with predominantly grey-brown plumage, darker on the back, crown and hind-neck, and is generally darker than the similar **Grey Teal**. It is sedentary, in small flocks, often with **Grey Teal** and occurs in coastal areas and inland waterways, from about Innisfail, Queensland, south through Tasmania and South Australia, to about Geraldton, Western Australia.

Hardhead *Aythya australis* 41-55cm

Dick Whitford

The male Hardhead, or White-eyed Duck, is easily identified by its overall dark brown plumage, white-tipped bill and conspicuous white eyes. The female's eyes are brown. Food, mostly molluscs, crustaceans and aquatic insects, is caught during deep underwater dives, which may last some time. The Hardhead is mostly silent, the only sounds uttered being a few soft whistles or croaks. It is nomadic and gregarious, forming small flocks on deep permanent swamps and lakes, as well as other wetland areas. It is most common in eastern and western Australia, occurring only as vagrants in the interior.

Australian Wood Duck *Chenonetta jubata* 42-60cm (Females smaller than males)

Peter Rowland

The Australian Wood Duck is identified by its brown head, grey and black back and wings, and speckled underparts. The male has a black mane, and the female has two pale lines passing through the eye. The bill is short and blackish. The call of the female is a drawn-out nasal 'gnew'; that of the male is shorter and higher pitched. A 'perching' duck, it seldom takes to the water except for bathing or mating. Most often observed grazing on a river bank or perched in a tree, this duck is a common sight in well-watered wooded swamps over much of Australia.

Green Pygmy-goose *Nettapus pulchellus* 30-36cm (Females smaller than males)

This is a beautiful little duck. The male is easily identified by its glossy green head, neck and upperparts, ornately barred green and white underparts and large white cheek patch. The female is somewhat duller, and can be distinguished from the similar female **Cotton Pygmy-goose** by its darker eyebrow and throat, and barred underparts. (The male **Cotton Pygmy-goose** has an almost entirely white head and neck.) It frequents deep lagoons and swamps, where it feeds on a variety of vegetable matter, often at night. A common sight throughout northern Australia.

Musk Duck *Biziura lobata* 47-73cm (Females much smaller than males)

The male Musk Duck has the unfortunate reputation of being the most grotesque bird in Australia. Both sexes are sooty-brown in plumage, paler below and becoming whiter towards the abdomen. The male is decorated with a large bulbous lobe of skin hanging from the lower mandible. The common name refers to the strong musk odour produced from a gland on the rump. It is usually silent outside the breeding season. Found in deep freshwater lagoons, interspersed with dense reedbeds, where it feeds on a variety of animals, from aquatic insects to fish and frogs.

Osprey *Pandion haliaetus* 50-65cm (Females larger than males)

G.B. Baker

A skilled fisher, the Osprey is predominantly dark brown above, apart from the white crown. The underparts are white, with a brown band across the upper breast and a brown eye-stripe, more noticeable on female. The undersides of the wings and tail are barred with brown and white. In flight, the wings are bowed and only slightly angled. The Osprey inhabits mangroves, estuaries and rivers, on or near the coast, where it feeds on fish, birds, mammals and amphibians. It is found throughout the coastal regions of Australia, except southern Victoria and Tasmania, and is most abundant in the northern part of its range.

Black-shouldered Kite *Elanus axillaris* 33-38cm

C. Todd

This is a small raptor. The upperparts are grey, with the exception of a large black patch on the upperwing; the underparts and head are white. When perched, the Black-shouldered Kite appears almost identical to the less common **Letter-winged Kite** but can be distinguished by a small patch of black feathers which extends slightly past the eye. In flight, it shows only a small amount of black on the underwing. It frequents woodlands and grasslands, where it feeds on small mammals, reptiles and insects. It is common in all but the more arid areas of the Australian mainland.

Black Kite *Milvus migrans* 47-55cm

R. Brown

The Black Kite is a large dark brown raptor. The tail is forked and barred with darker brown. The call is a descending whistle 'psee-err' followed by a staccato 'si-si-si-si-si'. The Black Kite is found in a variety of habitats throughout mainland Australia, and is often observed in and around outback towns. It is rarely seen singly and often congregates in flocks of several hundred, especially during grasshopper plagues. A bushfire is often the ideal place to observe the Black Kite, as it preys on lizards, small mammals and insects fleeing the flames.

Whistling Kite *Haliastur sphenurus* 50-60cm

G. Chapman

Although it feeds on live prey, the Whistling Kite resembles other kites in its scavenging behaviour and can often be seen feeding on animals killed on the road. Chiefly brown, paler and more streaked on the head, neck and underparts. In flight, the margins of the wings are darker, with a pale grey-brown wedge towards the tip of each wing. The underside of the tail is also pale grey-brown. The call, a descending whistle 'psee-err' followed by a staccato 'si-si-si-si-si', is similar to that of the **Black Kite**. The Whistling Kite is most common in open wooded habitats near permanent water.

Brahminy Kite *Haliastur indus* 45-51cm

This beautiful chestnut and white raptor is unmistakable. It is easily recognized by its white head, neck and breast and contrasting chestnut belly and upperparts. First-year birds resemble the **Whistling Kite**, but lack pale wedges on the underwing, and have a shorter tail. The call is a drawn-out 'pee-ah-ah-ah' or 'keee-e-yah'. The Brahminy Kite is solitary and pairs only during the breeding season. It inhabits coastal areas of northern Australia, from about Carnarvon, Western Australia to Hastings River, New South Wales, where it feeds on fish and other marine animals, normally stranded or washed up by the tide.

C. Andrew Henley/Larus

Brown Goshawk *Accipiter fasciatus* 37-55cm

This beautiful, slender bird of prey, should not be confused with the smaller and squarer-tailed **Collared Sparrowhawk.** Adults are identified by their grey-brown upperparts, finely barred russet and cream underparts and rufous collar. Immature birds are brown above, with broader brown and cream barring and spotting below. The Brown Goshawk feeds on a variety of prey, including birds, mammals and reptiles. It is generally solitary in behaviour. Although it is normally silent, some harsh chattering is emitted when alarmed. Found in most timbered areas around Australia, it is fairly abundant throughout its range.

Hans & Judy Beste

White-bellied Sea-Eagle *Haliaeetus leucogaster* 75-85cm

R. Brown

This unmistakable large bird of prey is a common sight in coastal and near coastal areas of Australia. Adults have white on the head, rump and underparts and dark grey on the back and wings. In flight the contrasting black flight feathers are easily visible from below. Young birds may be confused with the **Wedge-tailed Eagle**, but differ in having a paler head and tail and more steeply upswept wings when soaring. Food consists mainly of fish, turtles and nestlings from seabird colonies. The call is a loud 'goose-like' honking. Sea-Eagles form permanent pairs that inhabit permanent territories.

Wedge-tailed Eagle *Aquila audax* 87-105cm (Females larger than males)

R. Brown

With a wingspan that exceeds two metres, the beautiful Wedge-tailed Eagle is the largest of Australia's raptors. The plumage is chiefly black, with paler brown on the wings, nape and undertail coverts. In flight the wings are held upswept and the characteristic wedge-shaped tail is clearly visible. Pair-bonds are permanent and territories are permanent. It is normally silent, except for occasional whistles and screeches. Found in most Australian environments except dense forests, it spends most of the day soaring on thermal currents in search of live prey or carrion.

Peregrine Falcon *Falco peregrinus* 35-50cm (Females larger than males)

Reaching speeds in excess of 300 km/h, the Peregrine Falcon is the fastest falcon in the world. Superficially resembling the smaller **Australian Hobby**, the Peregrine Falcon can be distinguished by its blue-grey upperparts, black head, white throat and finely barred buff and black underparts; the underparts are more rufous in the female. The Peregrine Falcon is a swift and deadly raptor, feeding on small to medium-sized birds and, occasionally, some much larger than itself. Although it is found in most mainland and island environments, it is most common around coastal cliffs and rocky outcrops.

R. Brown

Australian Hobby *Falco longipennis* 30-35cm (Females larger than males)

This is a stocky falcon with long wings, dark blue-grey upperparts and streaked rufous underparts. The sides of the head are black, as is the crown in some individuals. In flight, the streaked half-rufous and half-white underwings are clearly visible and the tail is seen to be long and square (unlike that of the **Nankeen Kestrel**). Hobbies feed almost exclusively on small birds which they kill and carry off to be consumed either on the wing or on an exposed perch, high in a treetop. Hobbies are found in wooded areas throughout Australia, and are a common sight around urban areas.

L.F. Schick

Brown Falcon *Falco berigora* 41-51cm (Females larger than males)

R. Brown

The Brown Falcon exhibits a variety of colour phases. Generally, the upperparts are dark brown and the underparts are pale buff or cream. The sides of the head are brown with a characteristic tear-stripe below the eye. Birds from the tropical north are very dark, while those from central Australia are paler. The Brown Falcon is normally silent at rest, but utters some cackling and screeching notes when in flight. It is found in all but the densest forests, feeding on small mammals, insects, reptiles and, less often, small birds. Locally common throughout Australia.

Nankeen Kestrel *Falco cenchroides* 31-36cm (Females larger than males)

G. Threlfo

This is a slender falcon. The upperparts are predominantly rufous, with some dark streaking. The wings are tipped with black. The underparts are pale buff, streaked with black, and the undertail is finely barred with black and a broader black band towards the tip. The Nankeen Kestrel feeds on small mammals, reptiles and a variety of insects. Prey is located by hovering a short distance above the ground

on rapid wing-beats, the head and body kept perfectly still. It is found in most environments throughout Australia, but is absent from dense forests and most common in lightly wooded areas and open agricultural regions.

Australian Brush-turkey *Alectura lathami* 70cm

G. Little

The mainly black body plumage, laterally flattened tail, bare red head and yellow wattle around the neck readily distinguish the Brush-turkey from all other Australian birds. It inhabits rainforests and, occasionally, drier inland areas, feeding on insects and seeds and fruits, which it finds by raking the leaf litter with the large feet. Eggs are laid by several females in a single, large mound, approximately four metres by one metre, which is maintained solely by the male. This large, ground-dwelling megapode is found in eastern Australia from Cape York Peninsula, Queensland, south to about Manning River, New South Wales.

Orange-footed Scrubfowl *Megapodius reinwardt* 40-60cm

B.J. Coates

This large, mainly terrestrial bird is easily identified by its bright orange legs and feet, brown back and wings, and dark slate-grey head, neck and underparts. The head has a small brown crest. Calls consist of a combination of loud clucks and screams. Although it is the smallest of the megapodes found in Australia, the Orange-footed Scrubfowl builds the largest incubation mound, up to three metres high and seven metres wide. Inhabiting rainforests and dense vine forests, individuals defend exclusive feeding territories but several pairs may use the same incubation mound.

Stubble Quail *Coturnix pectoralis* 18-19cm

P.D. Munchenberg

Most widespread and well-known of the Australian quails, this small, mainly terrestrial bird is fawn-brown above, conspicuously streaked with pale cream, and has a bright red eye. It is paler below, blotched and streaked with darker brown. The male has a chestnut throat and a black centre to the breast. The Stubble Quail is much larger than the female **King Quail**, which it superficially resembles in plumage. The call is a clear, three-syllable whistle, 'cuck-u-wit'. The Stubble Quail is abundant in dense grassland throughout much of Australia but seldom observed unless flushed out.

Red-chested Button-quail *Turnix pyrrhothorax* 13-15cm (Females larger than males)

A. Young

This is a small, mainly terrestrial bird. It is grey-brown above with black mottling and conspicuous buff-white centres to the feathers. The female has a rich rufous throat, chest and belly; this is paler in the male and confined to the chest and flanks. In flight, two rufous patches are visible at the sides of the tail. A whistling 'churrp' is uttered when flushed. The Red-chested Button-quail is found in grasslands in eastern and northern Australia, from the Kimberleys, Western Australia to Adelaide, South Australia, and as far inland as Alice Springs. It is locally abundant, numbers fluctuating with food availability.

Buff-banded Rail *Gallirallus philippensis* 29-33cm

C. Seller

Generally observed singly or in pairs, the Buff-banded Rail is distinguished from other Australian rails by its conspicuous white eyebrow. It has mottled brown and white upperparts, banded black and white underparts and a narrow buff breast-band. Like other rails it is a

ground-dweller and is generally quiet and unobtrusive. The call is a loud 'sswit sswit', usually heard at dusk. The Buff-banded Rail is found in coastal and near coastal areas over much of Australia. Favouring thickly vegetated areas, such as mangroves, tussock grassland and reedbeds, normally near water, it feeds on insects and other invertebrates, seeds and some vegetable matter.

Australian Spotted Crake *Porzana fluminea* 18-21cm

R. Drummond

This large Crake can be distinguished from the smaller **Baillon's Crake**, by its all-white undertail and two-tone bill, which is olive-green with a red base to the upper mandible. Both Crakes are, however, mottled brown and black above, spotted with white, and have black and white barring on the belly. (The **Spotless Crake** is chiefly grey-brown with bright orange-red legs and feet. The **White-browed Crake** has no black barring on the underparts and has a conspicuous white eyebrow.) Crakes inhabit thickly vegetated swamps and lagoons, usually around inland rivers and estuaries.

41

Black-tailed Native-hen *Gallinula ventralis* 33-36cm

M. Seyfort

Bright orange-red legs and large, flattened, black tail distinguish the Black-tailed Native-hen from other rails found in Australia. The upper mandible is bright green, while the lower mandible is red. The upperparts are olive-brown, and the underparts are dark grey, tinged with blue. Some large white spots are visible on the flanks. It usually is silent, but will utter a short loud call if alarmed. Found over much of Australia, the Black-tailed Native-hen often occurs in moderately large groups, in open areas with nearby water and shelter.

Dusky Moorhen *Gallinula tenebrosa* 34-38cm

R. Drummond

Most of this bird's plumage is sooty-grey, browner on the back and wings. The feet and lower legs are green; the upper legs and knees are orange-red. The bill and frontal shield is orange-red, with a prominent yellow tip. Like other members of the rail family, the Dusky Moorhen is a ground-dweller, feeding on both terrestrial and aquatic vegetable matter, insects, molluscs and small fish.

The call consists of a variety of raucous squawks and whistles. It is common in freshwater swamps and urban parklands throughout eastern Australia and the far western corner of Western Australia.

Purple Swamphen *Porphyrio porphyrio* 44-48cm

This large rail is unmistakable. Predominantly black above, with a broad dark blue collar, it is generally dark blue below, with a white undertail (birds in south-west Western Australia are more purple below). The robust bill and frontal shield are deep red. The call is a loud 'kee-ow'; some softer clucking occurs between members of a group while feeding. The Purple Swamphen is mostly found around freshwater swamps, streams and marshes, where it feeds on terrestrial and aquatic vegetable matter, seeds, fruit and insects. It is common throughout eastern and northern Australia, with an isolated population in the extreme south-west of the continent.

T. Lindsey

Eurasian Coot *Fulica atra* 32-39cm

Dick Whitford

The Eurasian Coot cannot be confused with any other rail found in Australia. The plumage is entirely slate-grey; the white bill and frontal shield is diagnostic. Immature birds are generally paler than adults and have a white wash on the throat. Nestlings are downy, with fine, yellow-tipped black plumage, the head is orange-red and the bill is red with a cream-white tip. In Australia, Coots feed almost entirely on vegetable matter, supplemented with only a few insects, worms and fish. The most familiar call is a single, loud 'kowk'. Coots commonly inhabit vegetated lagoons and swamps.

Brolga *Grus rubicunda* 1-1.25m

I.R. McCann

Superficially similar to the **Sarus Crane**, the Brolga is a large grey crane, with a featherless red head and grey crown. Unlike the **Sarus Crane**, the red of the head does not extend down the neck, the legs are grey, (not fleshy pink) and there is a black dewlap under the chin. The call is a loud trumpeting 'garooo' or 'kaweee-kreee-kurr-kurr-kurr-kurr-kurr-kurr'. The Brolga frequents open wetlands, swamps and grassy plains throughout eastern and northern Australia. (The **Sarus Crane** is less common and restricted to northern Queensland.)

Australian Bustard *Ardeotis australis* M 100-120cm; F 70-80cm

Hans & Judy Beste

No other Australian bird resembles the Bustard. The back and wings are brown; black and white spotting in the front of the wings is most extensive in the male. The head and neck are grey-buff, except for the black crown, eye-stripe and breast-band (browner and less prominent in the female). The remainder of the underparts are white. If alarmed, a Bustard tends to crouch down on the ground with wings outstretched. When courting, the male's throat-sac inflates until it touches the ground. The Bustard inhabits open wooded grasslands, pastoral lands and shrub steppes over most of the Australian mainland.

Comb-crested Jacana *Irediparra gallinacea* 19.5-23cm

G.B. Baker

This striking bird gives a casual observer the impression that it can walk on water. In fact, it walks on floating vegetation, with the aid of its grotesquely elongated toes. It is identified by the red fleshy forehead comb; black crown, back and breast; brown wings; and contrasting white belly, face and throat. A faint yellow tinge can be seen around the eye and throat. Calls consist of a mixture of high-pitched squeaks. It is found in tropical and subtropical freshwater wetlands, from the Kimberleys, Western Australia, through northern Australia to about Grafton, New South Wales, being more abundant in the north of its range.

Bush Stone-curlew *Burhinus grallarius* 52-58cm

Hans & Judy Beste

The Bush Stone-curlew's small black bill, large yellow eye, conspicuous white eyebrow and grey-brown plumage, heavily streaked with black, distinguish it from all other birds. (The related **Beach Stone-curlew** has a much larger bill and has little or no black streaking on the plumage.) The Bush Stone-curlew is mainly nocturnal and reluctant to fly during the day. The voice is a characteristic drawn-out, mournful 'wer-loooo', often heard at dusk and during the night. Although more abundant in the north, the Bush Stone-curlew can be found in open wooded country, scrubs and even golf courses over much of Australia.

Pied Oystercatcher *Haematopus longirostris* 48-51cm

G. Threlfo

All oystercatchers have a bright orange-red bill, eye-rings and legs. The white breast and belly distinguishes the Pied Oystercatcher from the closely related **Sooty Oystercatcher** (which is all black in plumage). Oystercatchers feed on bivalve molluscs, which are prised apart with their specially-adapted bills; worms, crustaceans and insects are also taken. It is mostly silent when feeding, but may utter a whistled 'peepapeep' or 'pleep-pleep', when in flight. Commonly found in coastal areas throughout the Australian continent, the Pied Oystercatcher is rather shy of humans and seldom allows close approach.

46

Masked Lapwing *Vanellus miles* 33-38cm

K. Ireland

Unmistakable in both appearance and voice, this bird has predominantly white underparts, brown wings and back and a black crown. Prominent yellow wattles cover the face. Southern birds are black on the hind-neck and sides of breast, and have smaller facial wattles. (The **Banded Lapwing** is much smaller, and has a predominantly black head and upper breast, with a distinct white eye-stripe and bib and a red patch at the base of the bill.) The voice is a staccato 'kekekekekekek'. The Masked Lapwing inhabits grasslands, marshes and mudflats and, although common around urban areas, it is wary of people and seldom allows close approach. It is common throughout northern, central and eastern Australia.

Red-capped Plover *Charadrius ruficapillus* 14-16.5cm

M. Seyfort

This is a small wader. Brown above, reddish on the crown and nape, and with a white face and underparts, the Red-capped Plover cannot be confused with any other wader found in Australia. It feeds mainly on insects, which are caught on the drier shores of lakes, estuaries, marshes and beaches: it seldom wades for food. While feeding, a Red-capped Plover runs rapidly along the ground, stopping suddenly to snatch prey from the surface. The call is a faintly trilled 'tik' or 'twink'. It is a common sight throughout coastal and inland Australia.

Black-fronted Dotterel *Elseyornis melanops* 16-18cm

M. Seyfort

This small wader is readily recognised by its white underparts with a distinct black band which extends across the chest, around to the base of the neck and through the eye to the forehead. The upperparts, including the crown, are mottled brown. The bill is orange-red with a black tip and a conspicuous orange ring surrounds the eye. Juvenal birds lack the black breast-band. A metallic 'tip' is uttered in flight. The Black-fronted Dotterel inhabits margins of lakes, swamps and dams, feeding on aquatic insects, crustaceans and seeds. Found throughout the mainland and Tasmania, it usually occurs in pairs or small groups.

Black-winged Stilt *Himantopus himantopus* 35.5-39cm

M. Wright

The Black-winged Stilt is a large black and white wader with long orange-red legs and a straight black bill. It differs from the **Banded Stilt** in having black on the back of the neck and a thin white collar. The Black-winged Stilt feeds on aquatic insects, molluscs and crustaceans. Unlike the **Banded Stilt** and **Red-necked Avocet** it seldom swims for food, preferring to wade in shallow water, and seize prey on or near the surface. The Black-winged Stilt is gregarious and usually found in small groups on freshwater and saltwater marshes throughout mainland Australia.

Red-necked Avocet *Recurvirostra novaehollandiae* 40- 45cm

W. Labbett

Among the Australian waders, the Red-necked Avocet is distinguished by its russet-red head and neck, and thin upturned black bill. The body is white below, with black and white upperparts. The legs are long and pale blue-grey. The Red-necked Avocet feeds on aquatic insects, crustaceans, molluscs, worms and some seeds, which it obtains by wading in the shallows, sweeping its bill through the water in a scythe-like manner. It frequents shallow marshes and mudflats in both salt- and freshwater environments, throughout much of mainland Australia (absent only from the north-east).

Eastern Curlew *Numenius madagascariensis* 53-62cm

D. & M. Trounson

This is a large wader. The plumage is chiefly mottled buff and brown, paler below and on the rump; the legs are grey. The long sickle-shaped bill is brown with a pinkish base to the lower mandible. It can be distinguished from the **Little Curlew** and **Whimbrel** by its much larger size and longer bill (the Little Curlew is the smallest of the three). Curlews and Whimbrels inhabit mudflats, mangroves and swamps where they feed on molluscs, crustaceans and worms by probing their bills into the soft mud. The Eastern Curlew is a common sight around the Australian coast.

Common Greenshank *Tringa nebularia* 30-35cm

L. Pedler

This inconspicuous wader is a non-breeding migrant, mainly visting Australia from September to April. The upper back and wings are mottled olive-brown, paler on the head and neck; the underparts are white. The lower back and tail are white with pale brown barring on the edges of the tail. The legs are olive and the bill is dark olive-brown. The Common Greenshank's most common call is a ringing 'tiu-tiu-tiu'. It frequents inland and coastal lakes, feeding on insects and small fish, with a characteristic head-bobbing motion and is found throughout Australia (except the harsh interior of Western Australia).

Latham's Snipe *Gallinago hardwickii* 23-29cm (Females larger than males)

Hans & Judy Beste

Latham's Snipe is difficult to distinguish from other snipes that may visit Australia. The bill is long and straight, fading from black at the tip to brown at the base. The crown and back are mottled black and brown, with distinct pale cream markings. The underparts are buff-cream with distinct black barring. Its common call is a rasping 'khreck'. More widely distributed than other visiting snipes and thought to be the only snipe to visit southern Australia and Tasmania, it can be seen between August and April inhabiting dense, tussock grasslands or reedbeds in the margins of swamps and marshes.

Bar-tailed Godwit *Limosa lapponica* 37-45cm (Females larger than males)

D. & M. Trounson

This non-breeding migrant is mainly mottled brown above, lighter and more uniform buff below. The dull white rump and underwing, and long, slightly upturned bill distinguish it from the **Black-tailed Godwit**. Calls include a rapid 'tititi' and a sharp 'kuwit' in alarm. Godwits inhabit estuarine mudflats, beaches and mangroves, where they feed on molluscs and aquatic insects. Food is found by wading through the shallows or over exposed mud and probing the long bill rapidly into the bottom. This bird is common in coastal areas of Australia and Tasmania from August to May each year.

Sharp-tailed Sandpiper *Calidris acuminata* 18-24cm

C. Andrew Henley/Larus

The Sharp-tailed Sandpiper is a small shorebird. The bill is straight, dark-grey to black, with a paler olive base. The upperparts are mottled black and brown, with clear buff edges to the feathers, and the underparts are white, darker and heavily streaked on the breast. It is difficult to distinguish from the less numerous **Pectoral Sandpiper**, which has a more distinct separation between the breast markings and white belly. This Sandpiper inhabits shallow freshwater lagoons, estuarine mudflats and beaches in all but the most arid areas of Australia and Tasmania. It is one of the most abundant of the migrant waders found in Australia between August and March.

Curlew Sandpiper *Calidris ferruginea* 18-21cm

B. Chudleigh

The relatively long down-curved bill, grey upperparts, with white eye-stripe, and white underparts make this wader easily identifiable. In flight, its solid white rump, rounded tail and white-edged flight feathers distinguish it from other sandpipers. It feeds on molluscs, crustaceans, worms and insects, which it catches by pecking and probing in shallow waters. The

most common call is a soft 'chirrup'. Although found in some inland areas, the Curlew Sandpiper favours estuarine mudflats, beaches and wetlands, and is one of the commonest waders to visit the Australian coast, mainly from August to April.

Red-necked Stint *Calidris ruficollis* 13-16cm

T.G. Lowe

This beautiful bird is one of the smallest and most numerous migratory waders to winter in Australia. The non-breeding plumage is mottled grey-brown above, white below. In flight the rump is white with a broad black stripe extending from the lower back to the tip of the tail. The Red-necked Stint is very difficult to distinguish from other stints, but has a comparatively shorter bill and is generally plumper. The most common call is a faint 'chip-chip'. This stint frequents mudflats and beaches in both coastal and inland areas, where it feeds on molluscs and crustaceans.

Australian Pratincole *Stiltia isabella* 19-23cm

Hans & Judy Beste

This species is similar in size and shape to the **Oriental Pratincole** which breeds in Asia and visits northern Australia between October and December. The Australian Pratincole is distinguished by its dark buff-red breast and longer legs. The upperparts are generally light brown, paler on face, and the wings are edged with black. The black-tipped bill is orange-red at the base. In flight, the underwing is seen to be dark grey, lighter on the flight feathers: the feet trail behind the square tail. Most active at dusk and dawn, it feeds on insects. It lives and breeds in the arid plains of central Australia.

Silver Gull *Larus novaehollandiae* 40-45cm

K. Ireland

This is a small gull. Its white head, tail and underparts, grey back and black-tipped wings, easily distinguish it from any other gull found in Australia. The bright orange-red bill, legs and eye-ring are present only in adults. Juvenals can be distinguished from the immatures by a varied amount of brown on the upperparts. The Silver

Gull has a varied diet, ranging from worms, fish, insects and crustaceans to human refuse. The most frequently-heard call is a harsh 'kwee-aarr'. It is common in watered areas over much of Australia, and is rarely observed far from land.

Pacific Gull *Larus pacificus* 60-65cm

T. & P. Gardner

This is large gull. The back and wings are black, and the head, neck and underparts are white. The white tail, with a broad black band towards the tip, and the large yellow bill with red tip, distinguish it from the otherwise similar **Kelp Gull**. Young birds are predominantly dark brown and buff in plumage, the yellow bill and white rump becoming visible after the first year. It often occurs in small flocks, feeding on a variety of foods, including fish, molluscs and human refuse. The most common call is a loud 'oww, oww'. It is a common sight in coastal areas of southern and south-western Australia.

Caspian Tern *Sterna caspia* 50-56cm

G. Chapman

The largest tern found in Australian waters. The massive, bright red bill, with dusky black tip, and its large size easily identify the Caspian Tern. The body plumage is chiefly grey and white, with a conspicuous black crown, extending down the hind-neck. Food, mainly fish, is caught by spectacular plunging dives into the water, often from as high as 15 metres. Common calls include a deep, barking 'kaah' or 'kraah'. It occurs along the coast, as well as in wetland and riverine areas, throughout inland Australia (except the more arid areas of Western Australia). Most breeding takes place on offshore islands.

Whiskered Tern *Chlidonias hybridus* 24-26cm (Females smaller than males)

B. Chudleigh

In the non-breeding season this graceful predominantly grey and white tern can be identified by its short, shallow-forked tail, red bill and black crown, faintly streaked with white. During the breeding season, generally September to December, the underparts become dark grey, with the exception of the undertail which remains white. The Whiskered Tern is often encountered in small flocks, hunting for small fishes, frogs and insects over brackish or freshwater swamps, sewage farms and well-watered grasslands throughout much of the Australian mainland.

Crested Tern *Sterna bergii* 44-49cm

K.A. Hindwood

The Crested Tern is the second largest of the terns found in Australia and one of the most common. Its pale yellow bill and scruffy black crest distinguish it from the smaller **Lesser Crested Tern**, which is found only in the northern parts of Australia, and has a bright orange bill in the breeding season. Although often observed on its own, the

Crested Tern is gregarious and often forms mixed flocks with other terns or gulls. Breeding is colonial, on offshore islands. Most common calls are a raspy 'kirrick' or 'krrow'. Inhabiting coastal areas throughout Australia and Tasmania, it feeds mainly on fish.

55

Common Noddy *Anous stolidus* 40-45cm

N. Chaffer

Largest of Australia's noddies, the Common Noddy is identified by its dark brown plumage with paler grey crown. It is distinguished from the **Lesser Noddy** and **Black Noddy** by its thicker bill, two-toned upper wing and wedge-shaped tail, which is slightly notched in the centre. Noddies feed on fishes and squids, which they snatch from the surface of the water

in a series of swooping dives. Common calls of the Common Noddy include a harsh 'karrk' and lower 'kuk-kuk-kuk'. This bird is found along the Australian coastline from Geraldton, Western Australia, north to Rockhampton, Queensland.

Rose-crowned Fruit-Dove *Ptilinopus regina* 22-24.5cm

G. Threlfo

Although seasonally abundant and beautifully coloured, this small dove often goes unobserved in the densely vegetated areas that it inhabits. The rich rose-coloured crown, edged with yellow, and orange-yellow belly distinguish it from the **Superb Fruit-Dove**, which has a predominantly white belly. The female is duller than the male. The Rose-crowned Fruit-Dove is nomadic and gregarious, occasionally forming large flocks where fruit is abundant. The main call is a loud 'coo-coo-coo-coo-coo', becoming faster at the end. It is found in a broad coastal strip from the Kimberleys, Western Australia, across northern Australia to just north of Sydney, New South Wales.

Wompoo Fruit-Dove *Ptilinopus magnificus* 35-50cm

M. Seyfort

Perhaps the most beautiful of all the doves found in Australia, the Wompoo Fruit-Dove is distinguished by its large size, rich purple throat, chest and upper belly, and yellow lower belly. It has predominantly green upperparts, with a paler grey head and a conspicuous yellow wing-bar. Birds in the north are smaller. It feeds on a variety of fruits. The call is a deep resonant 'wollack-a-woo' and, occasionally, a more abrupt 'boo'. It is found in densely vegetated forests along the east coast of Australia, from Cape York, Queensland, to just south of Dorrigo, New South Wales, being more abundant in northern parts of its range.

Spotted Turtle-Dove *Streptopelia chinensis* 29-32cm

L. Robinson

The upperparts of the introduced Spotted Turtle-Dove are predominantly brown, with darker centres to the feathers of the back and wings. The head is grey, and the neck and underparts are grey-brown, tinged with pink. In flight the white-tipped tail found is conspicuous. Its large black and white patch found at the base of the hind-neck is absent on the **Laughing Turtle-Dove** of Western Australia. The most common call of the Spotted Turtle-Dove is a musical 'cocoo, crooor'. It is a common sight in cities, parks and agricultural areas of eastern, southern and south-western Australia.

Rock Dove *Columba livia* 33-36cm

D. & M. Trounson

Commonly referred to as the Feral Pigeon, this species is descended from the Rock Dove found in Europe and Asia. Many plumage variants have been developed by selective breeding over the years, the most common being a mixture of grey, black, white and brown, with purple and green sheens. The most common call is a moaning 'cooo'. The common and familiar Rock Dove is closely associated with human settlement in many countries throughout the world. In Australia it is found in large numbers in capital cities and larger towns, with the exception of Darwin. Birds have also been observed in many other areas of Australia.

Brown Cuckoo-Dove *Macropygia amboinensis* 30-43cm

N. Chaffer

The Brown Cuckoo-Dove is easily identified by its chiefly brown plumage, paler and more pink-grey on the underside, and long, wide tail. Females have black mottling on the throat and upper breast. Food consists mainly of fruits from trees and shrubs, such as mistletoes. It seldom visits the ground except to drink and consume small stones to aid its digestive processes. The contact call is a 'whoop-a-whooop', the last note higher pitched than the first. Although the Brown Cuckoo-Dove has been the victim of much habitat loss and widespread hunting, it is still common in rainforest and dense shrubbery along the east coast of the mainland.

Peaceful Dove *Geopelia striata* 20-23cm

The beautiful Peaceful Dove is easily identified by its plump stature, grey-brown upperparts, barred with black, pink-buff underparts and pale blue eye-ring. The black barring is more concentrated at the neck, forming a broad collar. The Peaceful Dove is common and nomadic, moving around in response to the availability of food and water. The call is a distinctive 'doodle-doo'. These doves are normally found in pairs or small groups, in lightly timbered grasslands close to water. Although absent only from the south-west of the Australian mainland, they are generally uncommon in the more arid inland.

M. Wright

Bar-shouldered Dove *Geopelia humeralis* 27-31cm

T. & P. Gardner

This slender dove is easily identified by its blue-grey face, throat and upper breast; its brown upperparts, heavily barred with black; and its rufous hind-neck. The remainder of the underparts are white, tinged with pink on the breast. Mainly sedentary, it moves around within a small area in search of seeding grasses and herbs. Feeding takes place on the ground. Its common call is a triple 'coo' or 'kook-a-wook'. This dove has declined in numbers following the introduction of the **Spotted Turtle-Dove** in 1870. It is found in coastal and near-coastal eucalypt woodlands and fringes of scrubs and mangroves, from the Pilbara, Western Australia, through northern Australia to Goulburn River, New South Wales.

Common Bronzewing *Phaps chalcoptera* 30-36cm

R. Drummond

The Common Bronzewing can be distinguished from the similar **Brush Bronzewing** by its pinkish-grey breast and paler brown back. Bronzewings get their name from the iridescent patches of green, blue and red in the wing. The male Common Bronzewing has a yellow-white forehead and darker pink breast. Both sexes have a conspicuous white line below and around the eye. Food consists of seeds and other vegetable matter, consumed on the ground. The common call is a deep 'oom', repeated several times. Found in all but the most barren areas and densest rainforests, the Common Bronzewing is one of the most abundant pigeons in Australia.

Emerald Dove *Chalcophaps indica* 23-28cm

Hans & Judy Beste

This beautiful dove is distinguished by emerald-green wings and dull purple-brown head, neck and underparts. Juvenal birds are darker brown, heavily barred with black on the head, neck and underparts. Although primarily a bird of the forest floor, the Emerald Dove often perches on the thicker branches of trees, where it feeds on accessible fruits. The common call is a repeated low-pitched 'coo'. Found in dense forests, mangroves and dense thickets, in a broad coastal and sub-coastal band from the Kimberleys, Western Australia, to near Bega, New South Wales, it is absent only from the Gulf of Carpentaria.

Crested Pigeon *Ocyphaps lophotes* 30-35cm

G.K. Taylor

This is a stocky pigeon with a conspicuous black crest. Most of the plumage is grey-brown, becoming more pink on the underparts. The wings are barred with black, and are decorated with glossy green and purple 'patches'. The head is grey, with a tall, dark crest and an orange ring around the eye. It is usually found in the vicinity of water, where it feeds on seeds of crops and weeds. If disturbed, it flies off with rapid whistling wing-beats, interspersed with short glides on slightly downturned wings. The common call is a wavering 'coo'. The Crested Pigeon is a common sight in lightly wooded grasslands in both rural and urban areas.

Spinifex Pigeon *Geophaps plumifera* 19-23cm

R. Brown

This curious little pigeon with a tall chestnut crest is distributed in two isolated populations within Australia. Both are predominantly chestnut, with conspicuous black and grey barring on the back and wings, and a black and grey line across the breast. The face is red, bordered with black, grey and white. Birds found in the Pilbara region of Western Australia have all chestnut underparts; those from central and northern Australia have a white belly. The most common call is a soft 'oom'. Both races inhabit arid grasslands and open stony deserts, usually in the vicinity of permanent water.

Pied Imperial-Pigeon *Ducula bicolor* 35-44cm

This is a beautiful black and white pigeon. The black flight feathers, lower half of tail, and spotting on the thighs and ventral area mar the otherwise snow-white plumage. Its food consists of fruits, plucked from the trees. In the late afternoon, continuous streams of birds descend to drink at nearby waterholes. The most common call is a deep 'coo-hoo', which can be heard from quite a distance. This pigeon is found in coastal and sub-coastal rainforests and mangroves from near Rockhampton, Queensland, through coastal Northern Territory, to the Kimberleys, Western Australia, being more common in the north of its range.

D. & M. Trounson

Red-tailed Black-Cockatoo *Calyptorhynchus banksii* 50-63cm

D. & M. Trounson

This is a large, black cockatoo. The male is easily identified by its dense crest of black feathers, almost entirely black plumage, and bright red undertail. The female is duller grey-brown, barred and spotted with yellow, and has a diagnostic whitish bill. The **Glossy Black-Cockatoo** of south-east Australia and Kangaroo Island, South Australia, has a paler head and breast and is much smaller. The contact call of the Red-tailed Black-Cockatoo is a rolling, metallic 'kreee' or 'krurr', usually given in flight. Commonly found in scattered groups and in a variety of habitats, it favours lightly timbered country along watercourses over much of Australia.

Yellow-tailed Black-Cockatoo *Calyptorhynchus funereus* 55-65cm

D. & M. Trounson

This cockatoo is easily identified by its predominantly black plumage, the feathers of the body edged with yellow, and its yellow cheek patch and yellow on the underside of the tail. (Until recently the **Short-billed Black-Cockatoo**, found in south-western Western Australia and having white tail panels instead of yellow, was considered a subspecies of the Yellow-tailed Black-Cockatoo rather than a distinct species.) The Yellow-tailed Black-Cockatoo's contact call is a drawn-out 'kee-ow'. Often seen in small to large flocks, flying on slowly flapping wings, it is a common sight in the eucalypt woodlands and pine plantations of south-eastern Australia.

Cockatiel *Nymphicus hollandicus* 30-33cm

P.D. Munchenberg

The plumage of this atypical member of the cockatoo family is chiefly grey, paler below, with a white wing patch, orange cheeks and a distinctive crest. The male can be distinguished by its bright yellow forehead, face and crest. The Cockatiel is usually seen in pairs or small flocks, in most types of open country, near water. It feeds on a variety of grass seeds, nuts, berries and grain, obtained either from the ground or from trees. Mostly silent, it utters a prolonged 'queel-queel' in flight. It is widespread and common throughout mainland Australia, especially in northern areas.

Gang-gang Cockatoo *Callocephalon fimbriatum* 34-35cm

L.F. Schick

The Gang-gang Cockatoo can be identified by its general grey plumage, each feather edged with greyish-white, and its short, square tail. The male has a conspicuous red, curly crest. It is almost completely arboreal, venturing to the ground only to drink or to pick up fallen food. It is easily overlooked when feeding. The most common call is a prolonged creaky screech. It inhabits

the eucalypt forests of south-eastern mainland Australia and northern Tasmania, being common in certain areas, but less numerous towards the boundaries of its range. It has an annual migration, moving to higher altitudes in summer.

Galah *Cacatua roseicapilla* 35-36cm

C. Andrew Henley/Larus

The Galah can be easily identified by its rose-pink head, neck and underparts, with paler pink crown, and grey back, wings and undertail. It has a bouncing acrobatic flight, but spends most of the day sheltering from heat in the foliage of trees and shrubs. The voice is a distinctive high-pitched screech, 'chi-chi'. The Galah is one of the most abundant and familiar of the Australian parrots, found in large flocks, in a variety of timbered habitats, usually near water. It occurs over most of

Australia and is becoming more abundant in areas of human habitation, where it is commonly seen swinging upside-down from utility wires.

Little Corella *Cacatua sanguinea* 35-42cm

M. Unkovich

Several races are found in Australia and are distinguished by bill length and body size. All are generally white in plumage (some tinged with pink), and have a conspicuous fleshy blue eye-ring, and a pale rose-pink patch between the eye and bill. In flight, a bright sulphur-yellow wash can be seen on the underwing and undertail. Birds from the south-west have a larger white crest. (The similar, but less abundant, **Long-billed Corella** has an orange-scarlet band across the throat.) Often forming vast flocks in trees along watercourses and where seeding grasses are found, the Little Corella is common and widespread.

Major Mitchell's Cockatoo *Cacatua leadbeateri* 35-36cm

D. & M. Trounson

This is a beautiful salmon-pink and white cockatoo. When the crest is erected it reveals a dark pink-red colouration with a broad yellow band running through the centre. In flight, the dark pink of the underwings is clearly visible. It feeds on a variety of seeds, nuts, fruits and insects, both in trees and on the ground. Forming small flocks, occasionally in the company of Galahs, the Major Mitchell's Cockatoo inhabits a variety of wooded habitats, especially mallee and acacia. The normal contact call is a quavering two-syllable screech. It is found in the arid and semi-arid areas of inland Australia.

Sulphur-crested Cockatoo *Cacatua galerita* 45-50cm

D. Greig

The white plumage, black bill and distinctive sulphur-yellow crest of the common and familiar Sulphur-crested Cockatoo distinguish it from all other cockatoos found in Australia. Although the normal diet consists of berries, seeds, nuts and roots, the Sulphur-crested Cockatoo has become a pest around urban areas, where it uses its powerful bill to destroy timber decking and panelling on houses. It is a noisy and conspicuous cockatoo, both at rest and in flight. The most common call is a distinctive loud screech, ending with a slight upward inflection. It is found in a variety of timbered habitats throughout northern and eastern Australia.

Rainbow Lorikeet *Trichoglossus haematodus* 28-32cm

This striking bird has one of the most beautiful plumage patterns of all Australian parrots. There are two distinct plumage variations. Birds in eastern Australia have all green upperparts, with a dark blue head, streaked with paler blue, and a pale green collar. The breast is mottled orange and yellow, the belly is dark blue, and the undertail coverts are green, edged with yellow. Birds in Western Australia and the Northern Territory have a dark orange-red collar and breast, and a dark blue patch on the upper back. It frequents open forests, rainforests and urban parks and gardens.

D. & M. Trounson

Scaly-breasted Lorikeet *Trichoglossus chlorolepidotus* 22-24cm

T. & P. Gardner

This medium-sized lorikeet is the only one to have an all-green head. The rest of the body plumage is green, with the exception of the throat and breast, which are scalloped with yellow, hence the name. The bill is orange and, in flight, the red-orange colouration of the underwing is clearly visible. It often associates in mixed flocks with the **Rainbow Lorikeet** and is common in open woodland and heathland throughout eastern Australia, from Cape York Peninsula, Queensland, to the Illawarra District of New South Wales. A small population of escaped or liberated aviary birds also exists near Melbourne.

Australian King-Parrot *Alisterus scapularis* 41-43cm

G. Little

The beautiful male King-Parrot is unmistakable with a bright crimson head, neck and underparts, green back and wings, and dark blue rump and tail. The female is somewhat duller and has a green head, neck and upper breast. The King-Parrot feeds on fruits, berries, nuts and seeds. The most common call is a shrill 'crassak-crassak'. It is commonly observed in moist and dry forests, open woodlands, orchards and suburban gardens. It is found in a coastal and sub-coastal belt throughout eastern Australia, from the Atherton Tableland, Queensland, to southern Victoria.

Red-winged Parrot *Aprosmictus erythropterus* 30.5-33cm

Hans & Judy Beste

The male Red-winged Parrot is one of the most spectacularly coloured of Australia's parrots. The head, neck and underparts are bright green, darker on the back, wings and tail, with a large rich-red patch on the upper wing. The lower back is bright blue, turning to pale green on the rump. The female is generally green all over, with a smaller red wing patch. The most common call is a metallic 'crillik-crillik'. The Red-winged Parrot is usually found in small family groups in open eucalypt and casuarina woodland, and acacia scrub.

68

Budgerigar *Melopsittacus undulatus* 17-18cm

W. A. Worrad

Although cagebirds have been breed in a variety of colours, the natural colour of the Budgerigar is green and yellow, with conspicuous black barring above, and a small blue cheek patch. The male has a darker blue cere. The Budgerigar is nomadic, taking to the air in a characteristic undulating flight. It is most active in the morning, drinking at waterholes and feeding on grass seeds, mostly on the ground. The contact call is a warbling 'chirrup', also 'zit' in alarm. It is found in most open habitat types, but seldom far from water, throughout most of mainland Australia.

Crimson Rosella *Platycercus elegans* 32-36cm

K. Stepnell

This beautiful parrot is easily identified by its predominantly rich crimson plumage and bright blue cheeks. The back and wings are black, each feather broadly edged with red, the wings having a broad blue patch along the edge. The tail is blue-green above, pale blue below. Young birds are largely green with varying amounts of red on the underparts. It has various calls, the most common being a disyllabic 'cussik-cussik', also a variety of harsh screeches and metallic whistles. Two separate populations exist within Australia: the one in northern Queensland is smaller and darker; the other occurs from southern Queensland to South Australia.

Eastern Rosella *Platycercus eximius* 28-32cm

C. Andrew Henley/Larus

This striking parrot should not be confused with any other parrot in south-eastern Australia. The head, neck and upper breast are red, with conspicuous white cheeks. The remainder of the underparts are yellow, washed with green on the abdomen, and red on the vent and undertail coverts. The wings and back are black, each feather broadly edged with yellow-green; a broad dark blue patch is present on the front of each wing. The Eastern Rosella's most common call is a staccato 'chut-chit'. It is found in a variety of open wooded habitats.

Australian Ringneck *Barnardius zonarius* 34-38cm

T. Howard

The most well-known and widely distributed form of the Ringnecks is the **Port Lincoln Ringneck**. Found in western and central Australia, it is identified by its green upperparts, black head, with dark blue cheeks, yellow collar and belly. The **Twenty-eight Parrot**, confined to the extreme south-western corner of Western Australia, has a splash of red above the bill and a green belly. The smaller **Mallee Ringneck** and **Cloncurry Parrot** are found in central and eastern Australia; both lack the black head and blue cheeks. The **Cloncurry Parrot** is confined to a small area between the Mackinlay and Gregory Rivers of northern Queensland, and has a yellow belly.

Red-rumped Parrot *Psephotus haematonotus* 26-27cm

This small parrot, subtly coloured with greens, blues and yellows is a common sight throughout much of the southeast. The male is generally green above, washed with turquoise on the head, paler green on the breast and yellow on the belly. In flight the red rump is strikingly obvious. The female is duller than the male, being generally olive in plumage, with a bright green rump and yellowish-white belly. Although generally observed in pairs or small groups, large flocks often form during the winter. It is commonly found in lightly-timbered and cultivated areas of south-eastern Australia, normally in the vicinity of water.

R. Drummond

Blue Bonnet *Northiella haematogaster* 26-32cm

The beautifully decorated Blue Bonnet cannot be confused with any other parrot found in Australia. The breast, neck and upperparts are grey-brown, the belly and ventral area are yellow, with varying amounts of red, and the fore-crown, face and chin are blue. When walking on the ground or perched, the stance is very upright. The contact call is a harsh 'cluck-cluck', often repeated. Common and familiar, it is found in lightly-timbered grasslands and arid shrublands in southern and eastern Australia. Small parties are often flushed from the roadside, where they forage for seeds.

M. Seyfort

Pallid Cuckoo *Cuculus pallidus* 28-33cm

G. Chapman

The Pallid Cuckoo is easily identified by its grey plumage, darker on the wings and back; and broadly barred black and white undertail. Immature birds are heavily mottled with brown and buff above, grey-brown below, with a darker breast band. The similar sized **Oriental Cuckoo** has conspicuous black and white barring on the lower breast and belly, and is generally darker in plumage. The Pallid Cuckoo lays its eggs in the nests of honeyeaters, woodswallows and flycatchers. The call is a loud, ascending whistle 'too-too-too...', repeated several times. This is the most common and widely distributed of the cuckoos.

Fan-tailed Cuckoo *Cacomantis flabelliformis* 24.5-28.5cm

R. Shepherd

The Fan-tailed Cuckoo is identified by its dark grey upperparts, pale rufous underparts and black and white barred undertail. The yellow eye-ring distinguishes it from the paler and smaller **Brush Cuckoo**, which has a grey eye-ring. (The **Chestnut-breasted Cuckoo** has dark chestnut underparts and less conspicuous barring on the undertail.) Eggs are laid in the nests of numerous other birds, including thornbills, flycatchers and scrubwrens. The common call is a descending trill, normally by the male in advertisement. This beautiful, slender cuckoo is often seen perched on an exposed branch in open forest or woodland, throughout eastern and south-western Australia.

Shining Bronze-Cuckoo *Chrysococcyx lucidus* 17-18cm

The beautiful bronze-cuckoos get their name from their metallic bronzed-green upperparts. The Shining Bronze-Cuckoo is identified by its white underparts with complete copper-bronze bars and copper-coloured head. It differs from **Horsfield's Bronze-Cuckoo**, which has rufous on the undertail and is duller above; and the **Little Bronze-Cuckoo**, which has narrow, incomplete bars on the underparts and a red eye-ring (males only). The contact call is a series of high-pitched whistles, often ending with a longer descending note. The Shining Bronze-Cuckoo is common in forests of eastern and south-western Australia and Tasmania.

G. Chapman

Common Koel *Eudynamys scolopacea* 39-46cm

D. & M. Trounson

This migrant cuckoo is often the cause of many sleepless nights and early awakenings. Arriving in September each year from New Guinea, the Koel advertises its presence by a loud ascending whistle 'coo-ee', monotonously repeated. The male is easily identified by its entirely glossy black plumage, tinged with blue and green, and striking red eye. The female has glossed brown upperparts, heavily spotted with white, and a black crown. The underparts are generally buff-cream with numerous fine black bars. Young birds resemble the adult female, but have a dark eye. It is found in tall forests and suburbs throughout northern and eastern Australia in the warmer part of the year.

Channel-billed Cuckoo *Scythrops novaehollandiae* 58-65cm

Hans & Judy Beste

Visiting Australia from New Guinea and Indonesia between August and October each year, this large cuckoo parasitizes the nests of several species, including the **Australian Magpie** and **Pied Currawong**. Its massive, pale, down-curved bill, grey plumage, darker on the back and wings, and long barred tail, make it impossible to confuse it with any other bird. It is found in tall open forests, generally where host species occur. The young birds do not evict the host's young or eggs from the nest, but simply grow faster and demand all the food, thus starving the others. The call is a loud 'kawk' followed by a more rapid, and fainter 'awk-awk-awk...'.

Pheasant Coucal *Centropus phasianinus* 50-70cm (Females larger than males)

C. Webster

Unmistakable. In breeding plumage, the head, neck and underparts are black, and the back, wings and tail are generally rufous, with black and buff mottling. The long, pheasant-like tail is duller and more brown in colour. Outside of the breeding season, the head and neck are straw-coloured, with paler feather shafts. Unlike other Australian cuckoos, the Pheasant Coucal builds its own nest and rears its own young. Its flight is clumsy and limited. The call is a distinctive 'oop-oop-oop-oop-oop...', descending in the middle and then ascending at the end. This large, mainly ground-dwelling, cuckoo is found in thickly vegetated areas of northern and eastern Australia.

Southern Boobook *Ninox novaeseelandiae* 25-35cm

The smallest and most common owl in Australia, it is identified by its dark chocolate-brown plumage above and rufous-brown below, heavily streaked and spotted with white. Young birds are almost entirely buff-white below, with conspicuous dark brown facial discs. The Tasmanian race is smaller and more heavily spotted with white, while birds of the Cape York rainforests are slightly larger and darker. The Southern Boobook is often observed perched on an open branch or tree-top, emitting a distinctive 'boo-book' or 'mo-poke'. It is found Australia-wide in a variety of habitats, from dense forest to open desert.

J. Hicks

Barking Owl *Ninox connivens* 35-45cm

This owl's plumage resembles a large **Southern Boobook**, although it is less rufous and more heavily streaked (rather than spotted) on the underparts. The eyes are large and yellow. The Barking Owl (or Screaming Woman, as it is often called) has two main calls, both distinctive and unmistakable. The first is a double-noted, dog-like 'wook-wook', the second a wavering human-like scream (seldom heard outside winter). Most common in savanna woodland, it is also found in well-forested hill and riverine woodlands. It is widely distributed and moderately common, although more often heard than seen.

F. Kristo

Barn Owl *Tyto alba* 28-39cm

Dick Whitford

Most widespread and familiar of the owls, the Barn Owl is medium-sized, with a 'heart-shaped' face, sandy-orange upperparts and white to cream underparts; both the back and breast are evenly spotted with black. By day it roosts in hollow logs, caves or thickly foliated trees, usually alone or in pairs. When threatened, it crouches down and spreads its wings. It is generally quiet, the common call being a 1-2 second rough, hissing screech. Found in open, often arid, country, such as farms, heath and lightly wooded forest, throughout Australia, it is moderately common but generally unobtrusive.

Masked Owl *Tyto novaehollandiae* 35-50cm (Females larger than males)

Jiri Lochman

Larger and generally darker than the Barn Owl, this species occurs in three basic plumage phases: pale, intermediate and dark. Upperparts vary from blackish-brown to grey-white, liberally spotted with grey and white. Underparts are rufous to white, speckled with dark brown. The facial disc is rounded and slightly more rufous than the underparts. It is bordered with dark brown, and the large black eyes are bordered with dark chestnut-brown. The call is a deep, rasping screech. The Masked Owl inhabits forests and woodlands in a broad coastal band around most of Australia, seldom more than 300 kilometres from the coast.

Tawny Frogmouth *Podargus strigoides* 34-53cm

When roosting during the day, the Tawny Frogmouth is easily overlooked. The general plumage of the common phase is silver-grey, slightly paler below, streaked and mottled with black and rufous. Another plumage phase is russet-red instead of grey. The eye is yellow in both forms. The **Papuan Frogmouth** is confined to Cape York Peninsula, and is larger, with an orange-red eye. The **Marbled Frogmouth** is similar in size to the Tawny Frogmouth but is found only in rainforests, and has an orange-yellow eye. The Tawny Frogmouth is nocturnal and common in wooded areas throughout Australia. It is larger in the south east than in the north.

N. Chaffer

Australian Owlet-nightjar *Aegotheles cristatus* 21-25cm

Dick Whitford

This delicate little bird with large brown eyes, is common throughout Australia. The Owlet-nightjar is the smallest nocturnal bird found in Australia, but, unlike other nocturnal species, its eyes are non-reflective to lights. There are two plumage phases: one russet-brown, the other grey, both paler below, and faintly barred with black. The wide black stripes on the head meet on the nape. By day the Owlet-nightjar roosts in hollow branches and tree trunks. Its call consists of a loud grating churr of either two or three notes, typically 'chir-chir-chir'. It is found in eucalypt forests and woodlands with suitable tree hollows.

Spotted Nightjar *Eurostopodus argus* 29-31cm

G.A. Hoye

The Spotted Nightjar is the only nightjar with an all-white throat. The plumage is largely grey, darker above, and spotted with buff, black and white. In flight the two large white wing spots are obvious. The smaller **Large-tailed Nightjar** of northern Australia also has white spots on its wings, but can be distinguished by its white outer tail feathers. Like other nightjars, the Spotted Nightjar is nocturnal, roosting by day on the ground, and resembling a piece of fallen wood or bark. Absent only from eastern coastal areas, it is common and widespread.

White-throated Nightjar *Eurostopodus mystacalis* 32-37cm

K. Ireland

Largest of Australia's nightjars, the plumage is grey-brown, more black above, and spotted with buff, black and white. The white throat is broken in the centre by a distinct black line. Unlike other nightjars, the White-throated Nightjar has no white markings on the underside of the wings or tail. It is generally abundant but difficult to see. The contact call is a laugh-like 'wook-wook-wook-wook-wook-ko-ko-ko-ko-ko-ko-ko', becoming more rapid and higher-pitched at the end. It is nocturnal and inhabits woodlands and forests throughout eastern Australia.

White-throated Needletail *Hirundapus caudacutus* 20-22cm

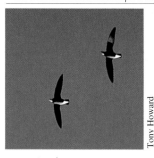

Tony Howard

This large swift is often mistaken in flight for a small bird of prey. Its grey-brown plumage, glossed with green, long pointed wings, short square tail, and diagnostic white throat and undertail, distinguish it from other Australian swifts. The much smaller **House Swift**, a rare vagrant to Australia's Top End, has a white rump and darker grey plumage. The **Fork-tailed Swift** has a dusky white rump and throat, but is otherwise uniform dark grey, with a long forked tail. Needletails often occur in large numbers over eastern and northern Australia, where they feed on flying insects.

White-rumped Swiftlet *Collocalia spodiopygius* 11-12cm

A.V. Spain

The most abundant swiftlet in Australia, this species is distinguished from martins by its reduced grey-white rump and more slender wings: the White-rumped Swiftlet is the only Australian swiftlet with a grey-white rump. The plumage is predominantly grey-brown, slightly glossed black on the wings. Both the **Uniform Swiftlet** and the **Glossy Swiftlet** are rare vagrants in Australia. The **Uniform Swiftlet** is grey-brown, slightly paler on the throat and vent, whereas the **Glossy Swiftlet** has a white breast and belly. Swiftlets are aerial birds, rarely landing, except when at the nest or roosting.

Azure Kingfisher *Alcedo azurea* 17-19cm

R. Drummond

This beautiful small kingfisher has resplendent violet-blue upperparts, rufous-orange underparts, paler on the throat, and bright red-pink legs and feet. A large buff-white spot is visible on the side of the neck. The long black bill is ideally suited to catching fishes, crustaceans and aquatic insects. The Azure Kingfisher is the second smallest of Australia's kingfishers, and is easily distinguished from the slightly smaller **Little Kingfisher**, which has white underparts and black legs. The Azure Kingfisher is found in stream-side vegetation and mangrove swamps throughout eastern and northern Australia.

Laughing Kookaburra *Dacelo novaeguineae* 40-45cm

G. Weber

This Kookaburra is generally white below, faintly barred with dark brown; brown on the back and wings. The tail is more rufous, broadly barred with black, and a conspicuous dark brown eye-stripe distinguishes it from the **Blue-winged Kookaburra** of the north; the latter having a blue tail and a large amount of blue in the wing. The chuckling voice that gave this bird its name is a raucous 'koo-koo-koo-koo-koo-kaa-kaa-kaa', which is often sung in a chorus with other birds; also a shorter 'koooaa'. The Laughing Kookaburra is common in wooded areas throughout eastern and south-western Australia.

Forest Kingfisher *Todiramphus macleayii* 17-23cm

Usually seen sitting motionless on an open branch or telegraph wire, the Forest Kingfisher is easily identified by its deep, royal blue head and upperparts and striking white underparts. Male birds have a broad white collar. Birds in eastern Australia are more turquoise and have a smaller white wing spot. A harsh repetitive 't'reek t'reek' can be heard throughout the breeding season, August to December. Forest Kingfishers are found in woodlands and open forests in a broad coastal and near inland band from the Kimberleys, Western Australia through Queensland to Taree, New South Wales. It is more common in the north.

C. Webster

Red-backed Kingfisher *Todiramphus pyrrhopygia* 20-24cm

Babs & Bert Wells

The blue-green upperparts, white collar and broad black eye-stripe may confuse this species with the **Sacred Kingfisher** or the **Collared Kingfisher**, but a closer inspection will reveal the distinct red back and rump that gives this beautiful bird its name. The underparts are white, thus distinguishing it from the **Sacred Kingfisher**, and the crown is streaked with white. It is generally silent for much of the year, but utters some drawn-out whistles and harsh chattering during the breeding season. Unlike the mangrove-dwelling **Collared Kingfisher**, the Red-backed Kingfisher is found in dry woodlands throughout most of Australia.

Sacred Kingfisher *Todiramphus sanctus* 19-23.5cm

Hans & Judy Beste

The Sacred Kingfisher is easily recognised by its blue-green back and crown, buff-cream collar and cinnamon-buff underparts. The upperparts are generally duller in the female and the underparts lighter. A broad black stripe extends from the back of the eye around the nape of the neck, in both sexes. The Sacred Kingfisher inhabits woodlands, mangroves and paperbark forests, feeding on crustaceans, beetles, reptiles and insects. The call is a loud, staccato 'ek-ek-ek-ek', repeated continuously at the commencement of the breeding season. This bird is common and familiar in all but the most arid areas.

Buff-breasted Paradise-Kingfisher *Tanysiptera sylvia* 29-35cm (Including tail)

Hans & Judy Beste

Early in November this beautiful kingfisher arrives in Australia from New Guinea to breed. Its blue, black and white upperparts, orange-buff breast and long white tail distinguish it from any other kingfisher. The bill is bright orange-red, as are the legs and feet. The **Common Paradise-Kingfisher**, with its white underparts and blue tail, is somewhat misnamed for Australia, with only one recorded sighting to date. The Buff-breasted Paradise-Kingfisher's presence is betrayed by a constant trilling call or a repeated 'chuga-chuga-chuga'. Within Australia, it is confined to lowland tropical rainforest in northern Queensland.

Rainbow Bee-eater *Merops ornatus* 21-28cm

Hans & Judy Beste

This brilliantly coloured bird is unmistakable in both plumage and voice. Both sexes have beautiful blue-green body plumage, a rufous crown, a yellow throat, and conspicuous black lines through the eye and on the lower throat. At a certain time of the year the two central tail feathers extend beyond the rest of the tail; these are longer on the male. In flight the wings are bright rufous-orange below. The call is a high-pitched 'trrrrp-trrrrp', mainly in flight. Bee-eaters are abundant in open, lightly timbered areas throughout Australia, migrating north outside of the breeding season.

Dollarbird *Eurystomus orientalis* 26-31cm

J. Bell

The conspicuous Dollarbird gets its name from the pale blue coin-shaped patches towards the tips of its wings. The plumage is generally dark brown, glossed heavily with blue-green on the back and wing coverts. The underparts are brown, glossed lighter with green, and the throat and undertail coverts are glossed with bright blue. The short, thick-set bill is orange-red, finely tipped with black. The Dollarbird's call is a harsh 'kak-kak-kak', repeated several times. It breeds in northern and eastern Australia during spring each year, migrating northwards to New Guinea and adjacent islands in February and March.

Noisy Pitta *Pitta versicolor* 17-20cm

A. Young

The Noisy Pitta can be difficult to see, despite its combination of chestnut cap, green back, iridescent blue wing patch, buff-yellow underparts, black belly patch, red undertail coverts, and tailless profile. In flight, it reveals large white wing patches. More often heard than seen, a Noisy Pitta can be attracted by imitating its 'walk to work' call. It will call in response or silently approach an observer and perch in a nearby tree. Various terrestrial invertebrates are eaten, snails being a particular favourite. It lives in east coast rainforests, spending much of its time on the ground.

Superb Lyrebird *Menura novaehollandiae* 80-100cm (Females smaller than males)

C. Andrew Henley/Larus

A lyrebird looks like a large brown pheasant. Only the adult male has the ornate tail, with special curved feathers that, in display, assume the shape of a lyre. The tails of females and young males are long, but lack the specialised feathers. The Superb Lyrebird occurs in wet forests of south-eastern Australia. The male's courtship display involves spreading its tail across its back while singing and dancing. The voice is powerful, and remarkable for its mimicry of a wide variety of other birds. **Albert's Lyrebird**, restricted to far north New South Wales and south Queensland, is more reddish, and the male's tail is less elaborate.

Welcome Swallow *Hirundo neoxena* c.15cm (Outer tail feathers longer in males than females)

D. & M. Trounson

One of several common Australian swallows, the Welcome Swallow can be recognised by its long forked tail, dark rump, rusty forehead and throat and light grey underparts. The **Barn Swallow**, an uncommon visitor to parts of northern Australia, has a black breast band and white underparts. The Welcome Swallow is frequently seen around buildings and other human structures, where it may nest colonially in open mud cups attached to a vertical wall. The voice consists of a variety of soft twittering notes. The Welcome Swallow is widespread in the south and east except for heavily forested regions and drier inland regions.

Fairy Martin *Hirundo ariel* 11-12cm

M. Seyfort

Both of Australia's martins have a short, square tail and pale rump. The Fairy Martin has a rusty-pink forehead and crown. The widespread **Tree Martin** has the top of the head dark blue-black except for a small rusty forehead. The Fairy Martin is gregarious, gathering in flocks to feed on fly-ing insects. A colonial breeder, it

crowds large bottle-shaped mud nests together on vertical surfaces, such as the inside of bridges and culverts. The call consists of a few soft churring notes. The Fairy Martin can be found in open country almost anywhere on the mainland.

85

Singing Bushlark *Mirafra javanica* 12-15cm

M. Seyfort

Australia's only native lark, is distinguished from other small brown ground birds by its short tail with white edges, chestnut wing patch and thick, sparrow-like beak. Its considerable variation in colour across its range is often correlated with soil colour. Eastern birds are dark brown, while northwards and westwards there are increasing amounts of cinnamon in the plumage. The introduced **Common Skylark** is larger and has a small crest and longer tail. An inhabitant of grasslands, the Singing Bushlark is frequently seen sitting on some prominent perch or performing its courtship flight, in which a bird hovers on quivering wings, singing loudly.

Richard's Pipit *Anthus novaeseelandiae* 16-18cm

A. Foster

Australia's only pipit differs from other small brown ground birds in its combination of prominent white edges to its tail, slender, pale bill, long, pale eyebrow and two thin dark streaks on the sides of the throat. It characteristically bobs its tail when walking. It is usually seen alone on the ground or perched along sides of roads, in paddocks and other areas with low ground cover. The usual calls are a trill given in flight and chirruping notes. This is one of Australia's most common birds, found throughout the mainland and Tasmania in grassland and other open country.

Black-faced Cuckoo-shrike *Coracina novaehollandiae* 32-34cm

Cuckoo-shrikes are slender, attractive birds, with the curious behavioural trait of shuffling the wings upon landing. As indicated by its name, this species has a black face and throat, contrasting with its blue-grey back, wings and tail; and white underparts. In young birds, black plumage is restricted to a mask through the eyes to the ear coverts. The call most often heard is a soft churring. The nest, a small cup, is remarkably small for the size of the bird. This species is widespread and common, and can be found in almost any wooded habitat and in many suburban situations.

R. Brown

White-bellied Cuckoo-shrike *Coracina papuensis* 26-28cm

J. Purnell

The most common of several colour phases can be confused with a young **Black-faced Cuckoo-shrike** but its black mask does not extend behind the eye. Less commonly, the face, throat and often much of the head are black, extending onto the breast as a series of broken bars. The voice is a churring, similar to that of the **Black-faced Cuckoo-shrike** but higher pitched. The **Cicadabird** utters a strange insect-like buzzing: the male is slate-grey, the female brown with a prominent eyebrow. The White-bellied Cuckoo-shrike inhabits woodlands from the south-east and east through to the tropical north.

White-winged Triller *Lalage sueurii* 16-18cm

I.L. Morgan

The adult male White-winged Triller is unusual in having two annual plumages. During breeding, it has a black crown, back and tail, and grey rump; the wings are black with white shoulders and white-edged coverts. The wings, tail and rump are similar in non-breeding plumage but the rest of the upperparts are brown. Females resemble non-breeding males but are browner on the wings and tail. The **Varied Triller** has a white eyebrow, black eye-stripe and light orange undertail coverts. The White-winged Triller's song is a clear 'ch-ch-ch-joee-joee-joee', ending with a trill. It frequents lightly wooded open country.

Red-whiskered Bulbul *Pycnonotus jocosus* 20-22cm

J.D. Waterhouse

In identifying the Red-whiskered Bulbul, the red whisker mark is diagnostic, but not easily seen. More helpful are the pointed black crest, white cheek, reddish undertail coverts and white-tipped tail. It is commonly encountered in parks, gardens and other suburban areas, feeding on native or exotic fruits, as well as insects. The Bulbul is not timid around humans, perching prominently on the top of bushes or on lines, from which sites it gives its characteristic descending musical whistle. In winter, birds may congregate at a food source. A native of southern Asia, this introduced species has become familiar in urban areas near Sydney.

Bassian Thrush *Zoothera lunulata* 25-28cm

G. Weber

Although common, this native thrush can be difficult to see. Its plumage, bronze above with white underparts, is boldly marked with dark scalloping, helping it to blend into the forest background: when disturbed, it stands motionless on the ground or a branch. In flight, it displays a prominent white wingbar. The **Russet-tailed Thrush** is slightly smaller with more rusty upperparts, and has a shorter tail. Shyer than the **Common Blackbird**, the Bassian Thrush prefers sheltered areas of moist forest, only occasionally entering suburban areas. The song is somewhat like the Blackbird: a series of pleasant warbling notes.

Common Blackbird *Turdus merula* 25-25.5cm

T.A. Waite

First introduced in 1862, this thrush has established itself in urban areas of the south-east. The all black adult male, with its orange bill and eye-ring, is unmistakable. Young males and females are less obvious: mostly shades of brown, with a paler, lightly streaked throat and a yellowish brown bill. The **Song Thrush**, also introduced, has a brown back and dark spots on its underparts. Not shy, the Blackbird is commonly seen on lawns and in parks. It is an accomplished singer, uttering a series of melodious phrases. Usually seen in urban areas, it also enters wetter timbered areas.

89

Flame Robin *Petroica phoenicea* 12.5-14cm

M. Seyfort

The orange breast and throat of the male of this aptly named species, and the grey back and white wing-bar, separate it from other robins. The female is largely warm grey-brown; however, the wing-bar is pale buff, and only the outer tail feathers are extensively white. Flame Robins pounce on prey from prominent lookouts in the open, returning to a perch to eat. The attractive song has been interpreted as 'you may come if you wish to the sea'. In summer they occur in forests and woodlands to 1800 metres, dispersing in winter to lower altitudes.

Scarlet Robin *Petroica multicolor* 12-13.5cm

C. Andrew Henley/Larus

The male Scarlet Robin differs from the male **Flame Robin** in having a red breast, and black back and throat (both have a white wing-bar). A pale reddish wash on the breast of the female distinguishes it from other brown robins. The male **Pink Robin** is pink below and has no white in the wing; the female has a double wing-bar and lacks white in the tail. Like other species, the Scarlet Robin pounces on its prey. Its song has been rendered as 'wee-chee-dalee-dalee'. It spends much of its time in woodland and forest, moving into more open country in winter.

90

Red-capped Robin *Petroica goodenovii* 11-12cm

M. Seyfort

This is the smallest of Australia's robins. The male resembles the **Scarlet Robin** in its black back, white wing-bar and red front but is distinguished by the red forehead. The otherwise light brown female also has a red forehead. The **Rose Robin**, a bird of moist forests, is pink below, grey above, and lacks white in the wing. The voice of the Red-capped Robin is a pleasant trill, rather insect-like in nature. This is one of the most widespread of the robins, preferring more open, drier wooded country than other 'red-breasted' species. It can be found in much of subtropical Australia, reaching the coast in many areas.

Hooded Robin *Melanodryas cucullata* 14.5-17cm

R.G. Palmer

The boldly marked black and white male can be confused with few other Australian birds. Any uncertainty is resolved by the black hood which extends onto the breast, the prominent white wing-bar and the white panels in the tail. The mostly grey female lacks contrasting body plumage but shares the male's wing and tail patterns. In flight, both sexes display a white wing-stripe. The male calls most frequently before dawn, giving a piping whis-

tle. The Hooded Robin prefers open, lightly wooded country across the continent. In Tasmania, it is replaced by the **Dusky Robin**, with plumage in shades of brown.

Eastern Yellow Robin *Eopsaltria australis* 15-17cm

N. Chaffer

Both sexes of this common bird are easily recognised by the yellow underparts and grey faces and lores. Southern birds have an olive-yellow rump; in northern birds it is brighter yellow. The **Western Yellow Robin** has a grey breast. The **Pale Yellow Robin** is smaller, and has pale lores and lighter underparts. The voice of the Eastern Yellow Robin

includes high bell-like piping, a repeated 'chop chop' and scolding notes. Its habitat extends from dry woodlands to rainforests, and it is often seen in parks and gardens. It is approachable, and often perches on the side of tree trunks.

Jacky Winter *Microeca fascinans* 12.5-14cm

G. Chapman

Although drab, this flycatcher is an attractive bird, with plain brownish upperparts, pale underparts, a slight eyebrow and prominent white edges to the black tail. The **Lemon-bellied Flycatcher** of tropical Australia is yellower below, lacks white in the tail and spends less time on the ground. From conspicuous perches, it watches for prey, catching it in the air or pouncing on it. While at rest, a Jacky Winter wags its tail from side to side. The song is a sweet, continuous 'peter-peter-peter'. It inhabits open woodland, paddocks and parkland.

Golden Whistler *Pachycephala pectoralis* 16-17.5cm

D. Val

True to its name, the Golden Whistler is an extroverted songster and the adult male is bright yellow on the underside and nape. This contrasts strikingly with the black head and breast band and white throat. Females and young birds are strong singers but lack bright plumage, being shades of grey-brown with washes of olive-green or buff. The voice is strong, musical and varied, including a 'we-we-we-whit', the last note strongly emphasised, and a rising 'seep'. The Golden Whistler can be found in almost any wooded habitat, from rainforest to mallee, including parks and orchards.

Rufous Whistler *Pachycephala rufiventris* 16-18cm

N. Chaffer

The adult male Rufous Whistler resembles the **Golden Whistler** in its white throat and black mask and breast band; it is distinguished by rufous underparts and a grey crown and upperparts. Females and young birds are greyer on the back, usually with a pale rufous wash on the streaked underparts. The Rufous Whistler is a spirited songster, producing a loud 'ee-chong', a repeated 'joey-joey-joey-joey', and other musical notes. Rufous and Golden Whistlers can be found together but the former generally prefers more open habitats. Both species are inquisitive and can be attracted by squeaking.

Grey Shrike-thrush *Colluricincla harmonica* 22.5-25cm

M. Seyfort

Plain grey, with pale lores and underparts in the southern part of its range, it becomes increasingly brown northwards. Adult males are browner on the mantle. Young birds have varying amounts of rufous on the lores and wings. What it lacks in colour, this species makes up for in voice which is rich and melodious, exhibiting considerable variation across the country. Typical phrases include 'pip-pip-pip—pip-hoee', 'pur-pur-pur-kwee-yewl', and a sharp 'yorrick'. This shrike-thrush searches for food on the ground and on limbs and trunks. It can be encountered in most forests and woodlands.

Crested Shrike-tit *Falcunculus frontatus* 15-19cm

M. Wright

The laterally flattened bill of this species is used for prising off bark and opening leaf galls. The bright yellow underparts are like a **Golden Whistler's**, but the crest and boldly marked black and white head are unlike any other Australian bird. The black throat of the male is replaced by olive-green in the female. Shrike-tits search for insects by noisily removing the bark; the sound of this action is a clue to their presence, as is the chuckling 'knock-at-the-door' call and a drawn out, plaintive whistle. They are birds of eucalypt forests and woodlands and some drier inland scrubs.

Crested Bellbird *Oreoica gutturalis* 21-23cm

The ringing voice of the Bellbird, is heard more often than the bird is seen. The male looks like a shrike-thrush with an orange eye, and white face and throat, bordered with black from the crest to the upper breast. The female lacks the white front and black band, but is recognized by the black crest and orange eye. The males call prominently, but, because the voice is ventriloquial, they are often difficult to locate. The cowbell-like notes increase in volume, 'pan-pan-panella'. Bellbirds are to be found in drier inland woodlands and some coastal regions.

A. Selby

Black-faced Monarch *Monarcha melanopsis* 14.5-16.5cm

N. Chaffer

The prominent black face and throat, sharply demarcated orange belly, and grey wings and tail identify this species. Immatures lack the black face. The Black-faced Monarch's presence is betrayed by its distinctive 'why-you-which-yew' call. It can be seen foraging among the foliage or sallying out for passing insects. Migratory over most of its Australian range, the Black-faced Monarch spends its summers in rainforest and wet sclerophyll forests. In the **Spectacled Monarch**, also a rainforest species, the black extends through the face, the orange reaches the sides of the throat and the tail is black, with white tips.

Leaden Flycatcher *Myiagra rubecula* 14.5-16cm

J. Gray

The male Leaden Flycatcher differs from other flycatchers in its leaden blue-grey upperparts. Females are duller and have a light buff-orange throat and upper breast. The male **Satin Flycatcher** is darker and glossy blue-black above; the female is slightly darker on the upperparts and throat. When not actively chasing flying insects, the Leaden Flycatcher sits on a branch, rapidly quivering its tail up and down. Its calls include a harsh 'zzrip' and a whistled 'zoowee zoowee'. The species is found in a variety of habitats, from open eucalypt forests and woodlands, to coastal scrubs and mangroves.

Restless Flycatcher *Myiagra inquieta* 19-21.5cm

E. Zillmann

This striking flycatcher is known more for its behaviour than its appearance. Its glossy blue-black upperparts contrast with the white throat and underparts: the breast is often washed with a dark buff. It hunts insects in sallies from a branch and by pouncing. This latter action consists of hovering while producing an unusual grinding noise, like scissors being sharpened on a stone wheel. Another call often heard is a musical 'chewee, chewee, chewee'. It is at home in open forest and woodlands, often near water. Northern birds are smaller, and frequently inhabit paperbark swamps.

Grey Fantail *Rhipidura fuliginosa* 14-16.5cm

G. Little

Fantails are great aerial acrobats when they chase flying insects. When perched, the characteristic fan-shaped tail is held slightly up and alternately spread and folded. The Grey Fantail is dark grey above, with white wing-bars, broken eyebrow and throat, and a dark breast band. The amount of white in the tail varies regionally. The song is a thin but attractive rising whistle. This species can be found in almost any habitat. The rump, base of the tail and eyebrow of the **Rufous Fantail**, is bright rufous. It looks and behaves like the Grey Fantail but usually prefers thicker, wetter vegetation.

Willie Wagtail *Rhipidura leucophrys* 18.5-21.5cm

G. Little

Superficially like the **Restless Flycatcher**, this black and white species is distinguished by the black throat and white eyebrow. It chases flying prey in the air and can be seen darting around lawns as it hunts for insects on the ground. As it does so, the tail is wagged from side to side. Willie Wagtails are fearlessly aggressive towards larger birds. The song, often given throughout a moonlit night, has been rendered as 'sweet pretty creature'. Widely distributed in Australia, the Willie Wagtail is found in almost any habitat except the densest forests; it is common around habitation.

Eastern Whipbird *Psophodes olivaceus* 26.5-30.5cm

N. Chaffer

Although usually secretive, this bird is also curious, and with patience, the observer can obtain a view. Adults are olive-green, boldly marked with a black head and breast and a broad white patch on the side of the face. The head bears a crest, the eye is pale and the tail is long. The Eastern Whipbird is more often heard than seen. Its explosive whipcrack call is one of the most characteristic of the Australian bush. The male gives a long whipcrack, usually followed quickly by a sharp 'choo-choo' from the female. This whipbird occupies dense vegetation near the ground in wetter habitats.

Logrunner *Orthonyx temminckii* 17-20cm

T. & P. Gardner

The plumage of this elusive ground-dwelling bird is mottled rufous-brown and olive-grey, streaked with black on the wings, back and sides of the throat. The face is grey, as are the sides of the breast, and the belly is white. The female is distinguished from the male by the cinnamon, instead of white, throat and upper breast. Food is found by raking through leaf-litter on the forest floor, while the bird supports itself on its spiny-tipped tail. The common call is a repeated piercing 'weet'. The Logrunner is found in temperate and subtropical rainforests from Gympie, Queensland to Illawarra, New South Wales.

Spotted Quail-thrush *Cinclosoma punctatum* 25-28cm

M. Seyfort

Quail-thrushes are ground-dwelling birds. Within Australia there are four species, the largest of them being the Spotted Quail-thrush. The male is identified by its black face, grey neck and throat and white eyebrow and cheek-patch. The body is largely brown, conspicuously spotted with black. The female lacks the black face and white cheek-patch, having instead a white chin and buff-orange throat. The call is an almost inaudible series of high-pitched whistles, also some louder double whistles. It is found mostly in drier sclerophyll forests from southern Queensland to eastern South Australia and Tasmania.

Grey-crowned Babbler *Pomatostomus temporalis* 25-29cm

G. Weber

This social bird is the largest of the four Australian babblers, and is the only one without a dark crown. Sexes have the same plumage colouration but the male can be separated by its slightly longer bill. The plumage is largely brown, more chestnut on the breast, with a white throat and cream crown. The tail is tipped with white. The **Chestnut-crowned Babbler** has a rich chestnut crown and white wing-bars, while both the **White-browed Babbler** and **Hall's Babbler** have brown crowns; **Hall's Babbler** is darker with less white on the throat.

Clamorous Reed-Warbler *Acrocephalus stentoreus* 16-17cm

Hans & Judy Beste

This slender warbler can be distinguished from similar warblers by its uniform tawny-brown upperparts, paler buff underparts and eyebrow, and cream-white throat. The **Great Reed-Warbler**, a rare migrant to northern Australia, is almost identical in the field, the only difference being its slightly thicker bill. The call is a loud, clear 'chut'. Both the **Tawny Grassbird** and **Little Grassbird** are heavily streaked above; the **Tawny Grassbird** has an unstreaked rufous crown. Moving south in spring to breed, the Clamorous Reed-Warbler is a common sight in dense vegetation around freshwater swamps.

Golden-headed Cisticola *Cisticola exilis* 10-11cm

N. Chaffer

Cisticolas are distinguished by their rich golden plumage and pale pink-yellow legs. During the breeding season the male Golden-headed Cisticola attains a beautiful, unstreaked, golden crown. The female retains a streaked crown, similar to that of the non-breeding male. The song is a drawn-out 'zzzzt', also a repeated metallic 'link-link' and

a harsh 'zeep' in alarm. The **Zitting Cisticola**, an uncommon resident of Australia's north coast, differs from the Golden-headed Cisticola in having a white-tipped tail. Cisticolas, like reed-warblers and grassbirds, inhabit grasslands, normally in the vicinity of water.

Brown Songlark *Cincloramphus cruralis* 19-26cm

Adult male Brown Songlarks have a very distinctive plumage. The general brown feathering is deepest on the face and breast, the crown is greyer. There is a great difference between the sexes of this insectivorous species, females being considerably smaller and of paler colouration. When maintaining a breeding territory, males utilize distinctive song flights, the loud notes of the song being uttered while the male flies high overhead with wings held upswept from the body. The song is also performed as he floats down to earth and may also be given while perched on a stump, post or similar object. The Brown Songlark frequents open country and is migratory.

G. Little

Rufous Songlark *Cincloramphus mathewsi* 16-19cm

Although smaller than its near relative, the **Brown Songlark**, a pale eye-stripe and tawny-rufous rump colouration assist identification of this species. Dark breast streaks are evident in younger birds. The adult male has a dark bill; this is paler in the female and immatures. The Rufous Songlark maintains a strong song, the consistent notes being uttered when perched or while in flight. Perches include the upper limbs of isolated trees or the top of a post. Also like its near relative, it has a distinctive song flight but the outstretched wings are held in a lower attitude.

R. Brown

Superb Fairy-wren *Malurus cyaneus* 13-14cm

C. Andrew Henley/Larus

It is fascinating to watch a family group of these diminutive, gregarious birds. Adult males are the most vibrantly coloured of the family group. Their rich blue, black and grey plumage distinguishes them from the browner females and immatures. Displaying males may erect their back feathers over the wing coverts creating a blue and black appearance. Calls consist of a series of high-pitched trills uttered by both species, the males often extending these trills into song. The species occurs south of the Tropic of Capricorn through eastern Australia and Tasmania to the south-eastern corner of South Australia.

Variegated Fairy-wren *Malurus lamberti* 12-14cm

Males of this species are the brighter coloured individuals: blue colouration is restricted to the crown and sides of the head, and there is a rich chestnut shoulder patch. Immatures and females are brownish grey. All have a longer tail than the **Superb Fairy-wren**. Females of Northern Territory and Western Australian populations exhibit a blue-grey (not brown-grey) plumage. The call is

a high-pitched trill. Habitats include forest, woodland and shrubland. The species is widespread throughout the continent, being absent only from Cape York Peninsula, Tasmania and the extreme south-western corner of Western Australia.

White-winged Fairy-wren *Malurus leucopterus* 11-13cm

The male is spectacularly coloured, even more so when assessed against the backdrop of reddish soil in the interior. The cobalt blue mixed with white and brown is very distinctive. Females and immatures are less colourful. Like many other birds, it can be attracted to the observer if he or she produces a high pitched squeaking. On two offshore islands of Western Australia the male's rich blue colour is replaced by black. The call is a high-pitched trill. The species inhabits areas of lignum, saltbush, and other low shrubs.

103

Southern Emu-wren *Stipiturus malachurus* 18-20cm

J. Purnell

The sombre colour, streaked darker, is broken only on the male, which has a powder blue throat. A unique character of emu-wrens is the tail: the six tail feathers are barbless and their loose emu-like arrangements has given rise to the common name of these birds. Trilling calls are very low in volume and pitch, being difficult to hear, even when in very close proximity. This heath-frequenting wren is occasionally found away from these haunts, sometimes even in forest areas. Its range extends from south-eastern Queensland to Victoria, Tasmania, South Australia and south-western Western Australia.

White-browed Scrubwren *Sericornis frontalis* 11-13cm

C. Andrew Henley/Larus

The white eyebrow is characteristic: otherwise it is fuscous-brown with slightly paler underparts. Subtropical and tropical populations are more yellow underneath, males having an almost black facial mask. Other populations along the southern coastline have dark streaking on the throat. The call is an almost persistent chattering of notes uttered as if being disturbed. It is an accomplished mimic. This insectivorous species usually occurs in pairs low down in thick vegetation. It is common and widespread, inhabiting rainforest, open forest, woodland and littoral scrub.

Yellow-throated Scrubwren *Sericornis citreogularis* 12-14cm

Dick Whitford

The yellow throat and dark mask, fringed with white or yellow, are distinctive characteristics, easily seen in the darkness of the forest floor, where this bird moves about in pairs or small family groups. It seldom ascends high into the vegetation. The nest is a large pendulous structure suspended from a branch over a stream within the rainforest. The call is a pleasant series of ticking notes and the song includes

melodious whistles, interspersed with excellent mimicry of the vocalizations of other birds. An inhabitant of many forest types, the Yellow-throated Scrubwren occurs in two isolated populations. One is found about the Atherton Tableland, Queensland, the other extends from southern Queensland to just south of the Illawarra region of New South Wales.

Large-billed Scrubwren *Sericornis magnirostris* 11-13cm

G. Little

The light brown plumage of this bird is almost uniform but the large black bill is distinctive. It feeds in mid-level vegetation, higher than other species of scrubwrens, moving about as individuals or small family groups. It does not build a nest but expropriates one built by a **Yellow-throated Scrubwren**. This plain, unmarked species inhabits the interior and edges of rainforest along the east coast from Cooktown (where it has a white wing-spot) to southern Victoria.

Speckled Warbler *Chthonicola sagittatus* 11-12cm

N. Chaffer

The Speckled Warbler is cryptically coloured. Bold speckling over the body, in combination with the deeper intensity of marking on the head, adds to its beauty. Sexes may be distinguished by the colour of the eyebrow, females having a chestnut colour mixed into the black eye-stripe (this colour is often hidden). The Speckled Warbler lives close to the ground. Its nest, built on the ground, is difficult to locate. The egg is a rich reddish brown. A strong mimic that often confuses an unobservant watcher, it frequents areas of drier forest, woodland and shrubs on the eastern side of the continent.

Weebill *Smicrornis brevirostris* 8-9cm

M. Seyfort

Weebills of northern Australia are the country's smallest birds. The name refers to the very short, stubby, pale beak. Combined with a pale eye, slight eyebrow, and unmarked crown and breast, this separates it from thornbills, which it resembles and with which it often associates. In the south and east of the country, birds are light brown; northwards and inland they become increasingly yellow and paler. It moves in active flocks, feeding mainly by gleaning insects from leaves. The voice is 'wee bit' or 'wee willy weetee'. The Weebill is found in wooded areas throughout mainland Australia except the wettest forests.

Brown Gerygone *Gerygone mouki* 9.5-11cm

N. Chaffer

The Brown Gerygone is like other gerygones in that it lacks the coloured rump and marked forehead or breast of thornbills but it differs from other gerygones by its olive-brown upperparts, white eyebrow, grey face, buff flanks and black subterminal tail band. The **Western Gerygone** has a smaller eyebrow and white at the base of the tail. The Brown Gerygone is a small active bird that forages among the foliage of trees and shrubs. As it moves through the foliage, it repeatedly gives a 'what is it, what is it' call. Its habitat is rainforest and wet eucalypt forest.

White-throated Gerygone *Gerygone olivacea* 10-11.5cm

G. Little

Many gerygones are sombre brown birds. Not so this species, with its white throat and bright yellow underparts. This colouration, plus the white-tipped tail and white undertail coverts, separate it from its relatives. The **Fairy Gerygone** has yellow undertail coverts and no white in the tail and northern males have black throats and white whisker stripes. The White-throated Gerygone's voice has given

rise to the nickname 'Bush Canary': one of its special sounds is its musical descending song. It is often found gleaning insects while hovering outside the foliage in open forests and woodlands.

107

Yellow-rumped Thornbill *Acanthiza chrysorrhoa* 10-12cm

W. Taylor

A pleasant musical call combined with jerking flight, black forehead with white spots and prominent yellow upper-tail coverts identify this species. It is invariably found on the ground, moving in small parties. Areas frequented include open forest, shrub, pasture and grassland. Unlike many endemic Australian birds, it shows a fondness for introduced pines. A nest is constructed in the outer limbs of hanging branches. The bulky

structure often has a second, unused, nest on top, the significance of which is not understood. The nest is entered by a side entrance formed under a protruding canopy or overhang. The song is a tinkling whistle. The Yellow-rumped Thornbill ranges over most of the mainland and Tasmania.

Brown Thornbill *Acanthiza pusilla* 9-10cm

G. Little

This is one of Australia's many small brown birds. Characters useful in identifying this insectivorous species include the well-scalloped forehead, streaked throat, and dark eyes. The call is a pleasant 'tchit! tchit!', uttered when disturbed. It lives in a variety of habitats, varying from rainforests to woodlands, where it moves in pairs or small active family groups, usually frequenting the lower limbs and canopy, only occasionally feeding on the ground. The nest is constructed low down in thick vegetation.

Striated Thornbill *Acanthiza lineata* 9-10cm

The distinctive features of this small brown bird include a strongly streaked crown, face and throat. It has a more greenish tinge and paler eye than the **Brown Thornbill**. In open forest and woodland, it frequents the outer canopy and limbs and is often seen on branches, moving in small flocks or feeding parties. Like many other thornbills, it mixes freely with other small insectivorous species when feeding. The call is a soft 'zit' and the song is a high-pitched trill. Its distribution extends from near Gladstone, Queensland, to south-eastern South Australia.

G. Little

Southern Whiteface *Aphelocephala leucopsis* 10-12.5cm

Hans & Judy Beste

Whitefaces are somewhat like thornbills, to which they are related, but they have much stouter bills. The face pattern, from which they receive their name, consists of a white forehead extending to below the eye, bordered by black. The body is a drab light grey-brown. In flight, the broad black tail band and lighter rump are somewhat reminiscent of thornbills. The Southern Whiteface feeds on the ground in small parties, hunting for insects and seeds. Soft twittering notes and a 'tik tik tik' are the most usually heard calls. It prefers open, often dry, country with scattered shrubs, in which it takes refuge if disturbed.

Varied Sittella *Daphoenositta chrysoptera* 10-13cm

R. Brown

This species shows considerable plumage variation across its range. Depending on its location, a bird can have a combination of white, black, grey or mottling on the head; white or orange wing-stripe; and plain or streaked underparts. All have yellow upturned bills with a black tips, short tails and legs, and large feet. The Varied Sittella feeds on the trunks of trees and has the remarkable ability of walking along the underside of branches. The commonly heard call is a high-pitched 'chip chip'. It is usually found in active flocks of up to 20 birds, in most eucalypt forests, woodlands and inland scrubs.

White-throated Treecreeper *Cormobates leucophaeus* 13-17cm

K. Ireland

Like sittellas, treecreepers forage on the bark of trees but they cannot walk on the underside of branches. The common species of the east coast, the White-throated Treecreeper, has dark brown upperparts, white throat and upper breast, and flanks with white streaks edged with black. In flight, a buff wing-bar is displayed. The **Red-browed Treecreeper** is similar but has a prominent rusty eyebrow. The White-throated Treecreeper's repeated, high-pitched piping is a common sound of forests. It can be found in rainforest, eucalypt forest and woodland, working its way up the sides of trees in search of insects.

Brown Treecreeper *Climacteris picumnus* 16-18cm

R. Drummond

This is lighter brown above than the **White-throated Treecreeper**. Its head, throat and upper breast are light brownish grey, the remaining underparts have buff streaks bordered with black, prominent buff eyebrow and, in flight, a buff wing-bar. It prefers drier, more open country than the **White-throated Treecreeper**. It works up trees in the same manner, but also feeds on the ground. The 'spink' call is uttered singly or in series. In the west it is replaced by the rusty orange **Rufous Treecreeper**; in the northwest by the much darker brown **Black-tailed Treecreeper**.

Red Wattlebird *Anthochaera carunculata* 33.5-36cm

G. Chapman

The name refers to the fleshy reddish wattle on the side of the neck. Although diagnostic, it is often not easily seen, and identification relies on the grey-brown body with prominent white streaks, yellow belly, pale facial patch and long, white-tipped tail. It has several distinctive but unmusical calls, including coughs, a harsh 'yac a yac' and loud 'chok'. The Red Wattlebird occurs in forests, woodlands and gardens around flowering trees and shrubs. It is aggressive to smaller honeyeaters, driving them from food sources. In Tasmania, it is replaced by the larger **Yellow Wattlebird**, which has a longer, yellow wattle.

Little Wattlebird *Anthochaera chrysoptera* 26-30cm

D. & M. Trounson

As indicated by its name, this is the smallest of the wattlebirds; however, it lacks a cheek wattle. It is much the same colour as the **Red Wattlebird**, but is distinguished by the white facial patch that extends down the sides of the neck, finer white streaking on the body and, in flight, a conspicuous rufous patch in the wings: the belly is never yellow. Not as raucous as the **Red Wattlebird**, its voice is a mixture of notes, including a loud 'quok' and 'kokay kok'. It tends to prefer drier and often scrubbier habitats than does the **Red Wattlebird**.

Spiny-cheeked Honeyeater *Acanthagenys rufogularis* 23-26cm

M. Seyfort

Looking like a small wattlebird, this species replaces wattlebirds throughout much of the drier mainland. The unusual spines appear as a white patch on the side of the face; however, the dark buff throat and upper breast and bicoloured bill (dark pink base, black tip), are better clues to identification. In flight, it shows a white rump.

The voice is an amazing collection of odd sounds: a sharp 'kwok', an ascending then descending whistle, and liquid bubbling notes. It can be found in a wide range of timbered habitats, where it is often common and conspicuous.

Noisy Friarbird *Philemon corniculatus* 32-35cm

C. Andrew Henley/Larus

Friarbirds are large, ungainly, grey-brown honeyeaters with large amounts of bare (usually black) skin on the head. The Noisy Friarbird has a completely naked head apart from a small patch of feathers under the chin and a line over the eye. The base of the upper bill is adorned with a knob and the upper breast is covered with long, pointed silver-white feathers. When calling, it throws its head back, giving a raucous array of notes. A loud 'four-o-clock' is one of the more familiar. It aggressively contests insects, soft fruits, flowers and other food sources in open forests, woodlands and gardens.

Little Friarbird *Philemon citreogularis* 25-29cm

C. Andrew Henley/Larus

Smallest of the friarbirds, this species lacks a knob at the base of the bill. The skin on the face is blue-grey and there are grey-brown feathers on the crown: younger birds have yellow on the chin and throat. Less noisy than other species, it utters a curious 'arcoo'. It has the widest Australian distribution of the friarbirds, inhabiting a range of open forests, woodlands, scrubs and gardens. In northern Australia are two black-faced friarbirds with low rounded knobs. The **Silver-crowned Friarbird** has a silvery crown and throat. The **Helmeted Friarbird** is much larger with a brownish nape ruff.

Blue-faced Honeyeater *Entomyzon cyanotis* 24-32cm

N. Chaffer

Adults are aptly named for the large blue patch of naked skin on the face. In young birds this area is yellow-olive. At all ages the Blue-faced Honeyeater is distinguished by yellow-green upperparts, black nape, crown, throat and bib, and white nape band. Northern birds have a prominent white wing patch, obvious in flight. This honeyeater is a noisy, active inhabitant of woodlands and open forest. It also associates with human-modified habitats, and can become bold around camping areas and picnic grounds. The call is also distinctive: a loud 'quoit quoit quoit', with each note rising at the end.

Noisy Miner *Manorina melanocephala* 24-29cm

G. Little

A colonial species, the Noisy Miner is by turns aggressive, approachable or curious. Its bold demeanour is complemented by a 'cocky' appearance: black crown and cheeks, and yellow bill, legs and skin behind the eye, contrasting with the mostly grey body. The **Yellow-throated Miner** has a grey crown, white rump, and line of yellow skin on the sides of the throat. The Noisy Miner's name is well deserved: among the calls are a loud 'pwee pwee pwee' and piping 'pee pee pee' when alarmed. Frequenting woodland and open forests, it has also become well adapted to suburban situations.

Bell Miner *Manorina melanophrys* 17-20cm

N. Chaffer

More frequently called the Bellbird, this species is better known to most people by sound than sight. The olive-green plumage conceals it in the foliage, despite the contrasting yellow-orange bill and legs, and small scarlet patch of skin behind the eye. Uttering the familiar and persistent bell-like 'tink', Bell Miners also have a loud, harsh alarm call, given when they are disturbed. A squeaking noise by the observer will draw calling birds to within a few metres, permitting a good view. It is usually found in tall open forest with scrubby understoreys, where it forms colonies.

Lewin's Honeyeater *Meliphaga lewinii* 20-22cm

Dick Whitfort

This honeyeater has dark greenish grey colouration, interrupted only by the creamy yellow of a gape and the yellowish crescentic ear coverts. The sexes are similar in appearance. It is mostly frugivorous, eating berries and small fruits, but also taking insects and some nectar. The strong rattling notes of Lewin's Honeyeater carry long distances and instantly confirm its presence in an area. It is common in the wetter parts of eastern Australia, frequenting both rainforest and wet sclerophyll forest, often wandering into more open woodland. Similar species found in tropical Queensland may be distinguished by size and voice: ear covert shapes are also distinctive.

Yellow-faced Honeyeater *Lichenostomus chrysops* 16-17cm

M. Seyfort

This is a medium-sized, grey-fuscous honeyeater. Adult males and females are similar in appearance: young birds have buff rumps. A yellow facial stripe between two black ones, and light blue eyes are useful identification characteristics. A species with similar facial markings, and with which it may be confused, is the **Singing Honeyeater**. Size and vocalizations are handy clues to identification. Noisy flocks fly high over a variety of habitats. At other times the birds are found singly or in small groups. It's call is a 'chick-up', usually uttered from the canopy or limbs in forest or woodland. Migrations of the Yellow-faced Honeyeater occur through eastern Australia.

Yellow-tufted Honeyeater *Lichenostomus melanops* 19-22cm

G. Little

The general yellowish colouration enhanced by the bright yellow of the elongated ear tufts of this medium-sized honeyeater aid its identification. A distinctive black line from the lores to the front of the ears is characteristic. Southern populations have a crest on the crown. There are no sexual differences in plumage. It is gregarious by nature but occasionally moves about singly. In groups, it is quite vocal, uttering a series of single notes sounding like 'quirk': at other times it may be silent. The preferred habitat is riparian forest but some birds wander in the post-breeding period.

White-eared Honeyeater *Lichenostomus leucotis* 20-21cm

J. Handel

The overall olive-green colouration of both sexes of this medium sized honeyeater is washed yellow on the underparts. In combination with the grey crown, black face and distinct white ear coverts, the plumage is attractive and distinctive. In immatures the crown is more similar in colour to the back. Although of similar size to many other honeyeaters, the plumage pattern helps identification, as does the repetitive 'chock-chock-chock' calls. Solitary by nature, the White-eared Honeyeater is found in habitats ranging from heath and woodland to forest. When lining its nest, the adult female will often take hair or wool from other animals (including humans).

Singing Honeyeater *Lichenostomus virescens* 18-22cm

G. Taylor

The drab grey-fuscous plumage of this widespread honeyeater lacks sexual differences. Immatures are duller in colour and possess a buff rump. The dark facial stripe over a pale yellow one is a useful identification character. Like most honeyeaters it shows a preference for nectar and insects, often taking the latter in aerial pursuit. Despite its name, it is not a great songster but it has distinctive calls, one of which is a pleasant, repetitive 'prit-prit-prit'. It inhabits semi-arid to arid woodland and scrubland.

White-plumed Honeyeater *Lichenostomus penicillatus* 15-17cm

D. & M. Trounson

Like many honeyeaters this is a medium-sized bird. Both sexes have a pale yellow-olive colour combined with an almost unmarked face: a narrow white plume about the ear coverts not only lends a name to the bird but assists identification. Western populations are much paler than those from the south-east. Breeding and non-breeding birds differ in bill colour: black (breeding), and dusky with a yellow base (non-breeding). A gregarious species, the White-plumed Honeyeater moves in groups that freely disperse when feeding. The voice is a pleasant repeated 'chickawee', frequently uttered about a main food source. It is widely distributed throughout Australia.

White-naped Honeyeater *Melithreptus lunatus* 13-15cm

L. Robinson

This is one of several birds with olive-green upperparts, black head, white nape band and a coloured area of bare skin above the eye. This species has red eye-skin (white in the western population), the black of the face extending under the bill and nape band. The **White-throated Honeyeater** has blue eye-skin, white under the bill and nape band almost reaching the eye. The **Brown-headed Honeyeater** has a brownish head, yellow-ish eye-skin and cream nape band. The White-naped Honeyeater is common in forests and woodlands, where its sharp 'scherp scherp' call reveals its presence.

New Holland Honeyeater *Phylidonyris novaehollandiae* 17.5-18cm

This attractive bird is rarely still for very long, usually busily feeding at a flowering shrub or noisily interacting with others of its species. When it perches long enough, the black and white plumage, yellow wing patch, small white ear tuft, thin white whisker and white eye ensure identification. Found with this species is the very similar **White-cheeked Honeyeater** which has a single large cheek patch and a dark eye. The New Holland Honeyeater's voice comprises a loud 'chik', thin 'pseet' and chattering. It is common in heath, forests, woodland and gardens, particularly if grevilleas and banksias are present.

J. Handel

Eastern Spinebill *Acanthorhynchus tenuirostris* 15-16.5cm

N. Chaffer

This bird is unlikely to be confused with any other species. The orange-centred white throat, black crescent on the sides of the chest and orange belly are unmistakable, as is the long, fine curved bill. The **Western Spinebill** has an entirely orange throat, white belly and white eyebrow. Spinebills are active birds, and often hover when feeding on nectar. In flight, the outer white tail feathers are prominent and the wingbeat is noisy. The mostly frequently heard call is a high staccato piping. The Eastern Spinebill occurs around flowers in forests, woodlands, heaths and gardens.

Scarlet Honeyeater *Myzomela sanguinolenta* 10-11cm

G.A. Hoye

This bird is diminutive in size but not in colour or voice. The male has a vibrant scarlet head and central back over a black back, breast and tail: the female and young are brown. Its decurved bill helps identification. It feeds on nectar, insects and fruits and is attracted to flowering urban shrubs. The voice is a pleasant high-pitched warble, short in duration, often heard in forest or riparian situations. Ranging from north Queensland to Victoria, it is resident in the north and an irregular visitor in the south.

White-fronted Chat *Epthianura albifrons* 11-13cm

R. Drummond

This small bird has black and white colouration. Especially characteristic of the male chat is the black cap over a white facial area and a black breast-band. Females and immatures are a grey-fuscous colour with a reduced breast-band. It differs from the smaller **Double-barred Finch** in having a longer, finer bill, and a single breast-band (not double). In flight it shows a distinctive dark tail, edged with white. The quiet 'tang' call is characteristic of the species. The White-fronted Chat inhabits open areas of low vegetation, especially about wetlands. Although widely distributed, it appears to be declining.

Crimson Chat *Epthianura tricolor* 10-12cm

The brilliant crimson, white, and black plumage of this male chat is diagnostic. Females and immatures are drab in comparison, being brownish and having a washed out redness on the rump and breast. Another red-coloured bird with which it could be confused is the **Red-capped Robin**. Much time is spent feeding on the ground and in low shrubbery. It is frequently seen in loose flocks, and often in smaller groups. Vocalizations vary from simple single notes to a repetitive 'dik-it' or trills. The species is nomadic, inhabiting dry open environments throughout most of Australia.

M. Willis

Yellow-bellied Sunbird *Nectarinia jugularis* 10-12cm

Australia's only sunbird is a familiar bird of the tropical north-eastern coast. The long curved bill resembles that of some honeyeaters but the bright yellow underparts prevent any confusion. Yellow colouration extends to the throat and upper breast of the female but is replaced in the adult male by glossy blue-black feathers. The Sunbird hovers to take nectar from flowers and shows a liking for spiders. High-pitched notes are given in flight and display. It can be found along the edges of rainforests and in suburban parks and gardens. Nests are often built round houses, where individuals become less wary of humans.

K. Ireland

Mistletoebird *Dicaeum hirundinaceum* 10-11cm

R. Brown

This is one of the country's smallest birds. The adult male's glossy blue-black upperparts and wings, red throat and undertail coverts, and black stripe down the centre of the belly are diagnostic. The drably coloured female and young birds are less obvious but can be identified by the pink undertail coverts. The food is mostly mistletoe berries. The Mistletoebird's sticky droppings, containing seeds of this parasitic plant adhere to tree branches and help to spread it. The most commonly heard call is a short 'wit' given while in flight. This bird is found in any habitat throughout mainland Australia where mistletoes are present.

Spotted Pardalote *Pardalotus punctatus* 8-9.5cm

T. & P. Gardner

Although common, this species frequently passes unnoticed because it spends most of its time near the tops of trees. Seen closely, it is a striking bird. The male has fine white spots on the black crown and wings, a yellow throat and undertail coverts, and a reddish chestnut rump. The female is duller, with an off-white throat and cream spots on the crown. The most obvious indication of its presence is the frequently repeated, somewhat bell-like 'sleep ba-bee'. This pardalote can be found in most wooded habitats, including suburban parks. The nest is made in a tunnel in an earthen bank.

Striated Pardalote *Pardalotus striatus* 9.5-11cm

Like the **Spotted Pardalote**, this species is more common than is usually realized. Across Australia, it has white eyebrow with a yellow spot in front of the eye, an olive-grey back and a white stripe in the wing. Other colouration is very variable. The wing stripe may be narrow or wide, with a red or yellow spot at the front end of it. The crown is black, with or without fine white stripes. A frequent call is a sharp 'tchip tchip'. This pardalote can be found in almost any habitat with trees or shrubs.

G. Little

Silvereye *Zosterops lateralis* 9.5-12cm

D. & M. Trounson

This is one of a group of birds known as white-eyes because of the conspicuous ring of white feathers around the eye. The Silvereye exhibits interesting plumage variations across its range. The grey back and olive-green head and wings are found in birds throughout the east; western birds have the back uniformly olive-green. Breeding birds of the east coast have yellow throats, pale buff flanks and white undertail coverts. During winter, these are replaced by southern birds, which have grey throats, chestnut flanks and yellow undertail coverts. The contact call, a thin 'psip', is given continually. Silvereyes may occur in almost any wooded habitat.

House Sparrow *Passer domesticus* 14-16cm

B. Chudleigh

Following its introduction between 1863 and 1870, the House Sparrow quickly established itself in urban settlements throughout eastern Australia. The male is conspicuous with its grey crown, black face and throat and dark black and brown upperparts. The remainder of the underparts are pale grey-brown. The female is slightly paler and lacks the grey crown and black face, instead having a pale buff eye-stripe. Both the male and female **Tree Sparrow**, found only in south-eastern Australia, are similar to the male House Sparrow, but they have an all-brown crown and black ear patch. The call is a harsh 'cheer-up'.

Goldfinch *Carduelis carduelis* 12-15cm

N. Chaffer

This small, brightly-coloured finch, with a striking red facial disc, was introduced into Australia in the 1850s and quickly became established in the south-east. A few isolated populations in areas around Perth and Albany, Western Australia, are descended from escaped or liberated aviary birds. The plumage is largely buff above with a white rump, and black and golden-yellow wings. The underparts are white with varying amounts of buff, and the crown to nape is black. Goldfinches are gregarious, found throughout the year in small groups called 'charms', but occasionally flocks of 500 or more birds are seen. The common call is a repeated 'swilt-witt-witt'.

Red-browed Finch *Neochmia temporalis* 10-12cm

N. Chaffer

Like a fiery dart as it flies, this medium-sized finch is distinguished from other Australian finches, by its bright red rump and eyebrow. The remainder of the upperparts are olive-green, and the underparts and head are grey. The bill is red with a broad black wedge on the top and bottom mandible. The call is a high-pitched 'seeee' or 'ssitt'. It is found in a variety of habitats, especially shrublands with open grassy areas. The Red-browed Finch is distributed in a broad coastal band along the east coast, from Cape York, Queensland, to Adelaide, South Australia. A small population also exists near Perth, Western Australia.

Zebra Finch *Taeniopygia guttata* 10-11.5cm

Hans & Judy Beste

Generally associated with the more arid areas of Australia, the Zebra Finch is the most common and widespread of Australia's finches. The plumage is generally grey, with characteristic black 'tear-drop' eyestripes and 'zebra-like' black and white barring on rump and uppertail. The male is distinguished from the female by its conspicuous chestnut cheeks. The most common calls are a loud nasal 'tiah', often given in flight, and a soft 'tet-tet' in close contact. Zebra Finches live year round in social flocks of 10 to 100 birds in a variety of habitats, mainly dry wooded grasslands, bordering watercourses.

Double-barred Finch *Taeniopygia bichenovii* 9.5-11.5cm

N. Chaffer

Double-barred Finches need to drink regularly and are seldom found far from permanent water. Both sexes have a white face and cheeks, bordered with a broad black line. The white upper-breast is separated from the buff-white belly by another broad black line, and the upperparts are generally brown, heavily spotted with white on the wings. Birds from west of the Gulf of Carpentaria have a black, instead of white, rump. Double-barred Finches inhabit grassy thickets in open woodland and forest, from the Kimberleys, Western Australia, across the north, then south to Victoria. They usually occur in flocks of up to 30 or 40 birds.

Crimson Finch *Neochmia phaeton* 12-14cm

D. & M. Trounson

This large finch with a long, tapered red tail and red face cannot be confused with any other Australian finch. The upperparts are brown, washed with grey and red. The underparts are pale brown on the female, crimson on the male. Birds from Cape York Peninsula have a white belly. The Crimson Finch is not especially gregarious, usually occurring alone or in family groups, but will mix with other finch flocks. The call, a loud, penetrating 'tsee-tsee-tsee-tsee-tsee', can be heard over several hundred metres. It inhabits pockets of tall grassland and pandanus.

Chestnut-breasted Mannikin *Lonchura castaneothorax* 10-12.5cm

This beautiful, thick-set finch, with a powerful bill, is highly social, often forming vast flocks of several hundred birds. The upperparts are rich chestnut, with a grey crown. The underparts are generally white, with a broad chestnut breast-band, bordered below with black, and a conspicuous black face and throat. The call, 'teet' or 'tit', which may be either bell-like or long and drawn-out, is used in a variety of situations. The song, however, is long and high-pitched, often lasting up to 12 seconds. It is common in rank grasses and reeds, from the Kimberleys, Western Australia, to Sydney, New South Wales.

Hans & Judy Beste

Metallic Starling *Aplonis metallica* 21.5-24cm

Australia's only native starling lacks the disagreeable habits of its introduced relatives. Adults are entirely glossy oily black with long pointed tails and large bright red eyes. Young birds are similar except for the white throat and underparts, streaked with black. This species is colonial, and birds of different ages are seen together, particularly at nest trees, where their hanging nests are clustered in the outer branches. Food includes insects and introduced fruits. The voice includes chattering notes and a canary-like song. It is a bird of rainforests, mangroves and developed areas, where it becomes tame, often nesting in towns.

Hans & Judy Beste

127

Common Starling *Sturnus vulgaris* 20-22cm

Babs & Bert Wells

Introduced in the 1860s, this species has become well established and is expanding its range. When the plumage is fresh, the tips of the glossy purple-black body feathers sport large white spots. At this time the bill is dark. With wear, the white spots are lost, producing an unmarked plumage, and the bill turns yellow. Young birds are dull brown. The song is an unmusical collection of wheezy whistles, clicks, scratching notes and some mimicry. It is usually found near human habitation and most often seen when searching for seeds and insects on lawns and in paddocks. It also raids fruit crops.

Common Myna *Acridotheres tristis* 23-25.5cm

K. Griffiths

This bird, which was introduced in the 1860s and is now a serious pest, could be confused with the Noisy Miner, a native honeyeater. Both have yellow bills, legs and bare eye skin, but the Myna is brown with a black head. In flight, it shows large white wing patches. It is aggressive towards other species, bullying them around food sources and usurping nesting recesses. The voice is unpleasant: a collection of growls and other harsh notes. It is closely associated with towns and cities, rarely moving far from habitation, where it searches for natural food and human scraps.

Olive-backed Oriole *Oriolus sagittatus* 26-28cm

C. Andrew Henley

Although similar in size to several other species that gather together in fruiting trees, the Olive-backed Oriole is recognized by the combination of olive-green upperparts, white underparts with dark teardrop-shaped streaks and, in particular, the salmon-coloured bill. The red eye is a further clue. The **Yellow Oriole** of tropical Australia is yellow-green and more finely streaked below. The Olive-backed Oriole's pleasant 'olly ole' call is a feature of its habitats. It feeds on insects and a variety of soft fruits, which it finds in wooded areas from rainforest to some drier inland scrubs and in orchards and gardens.

Figbird *Sphecotheres viridis* 27.5-29cm

Hans & Judy Beste

Frequently associating with the **Olive-backed Oriole**, the Figbird can also be confused with it. Females are superficially oriole-like but have dark brown upperparts, more heavily streaked underparts, a short dark bill and dark eye. Males present no difficulties. The back is olive-green, head black and the eye is surrounded by naked red skin. Southern birds have grey underparts and collar; northern ones are bright yellow below and lack the grey collar. Females are similar throughout their range. As its name suggests, the Figbird largely eats soft fruits. It lives in flocks in rainforest and eucalypt forest, where its downwardly inflected 'tcher' is a characteristic background sound.

Spangled Drongo *Dicrurus bracteatus* 28-32cm (Females smaller than males)

R. Vitjoen

The glossy black plumage and blood-red eye are striking, but the characteristic long, forked 'fish' tail confirms the identification of this species. The Spangled Drongo is noisy and conspicuous, usually active, and frequently aggressive to other species. It sits on a prominent perch, from which it dashes out to capture passing insects. It also gleens insects from bark and foliage, and will take nectar from flowers. The voice comprises a variety of sounds, including some distinctive metallic notes like a stretched wire being plucked. Although preferring wetter forests, it can also be found in other woodlands, mangroves and parks.

Satin Bowerbird *Ptilonorhynchus violaceus* 27-33cm

L.F. Schick

The adult male takes seven years to acquire its glossy blue-black plumage, pale bill and violet-blue iris. Younger males resemble the female in being olive-green above, off-white with dark scalloping below, with brown wings and tail: the bill and iris are dark brown. While adult males are solitary, 'green' birds frequently form large flocks. There is an amazing variety of calls, some mechanical in nature, as well as mimicry. The male gives a loud 'weeoo'. The bower, consisting of two parallel walls of sticks, is built on the ground in wetter forests and woodlands. In winter, birds move to more open country.

Regent Bowerbird *Sericulus chrysocephalus* 24-28cm

Few birds can compare with the adult male: its golden wings, shoulders, nape, crown, iris and bill contrast strikingly with the otherwise black plumage. Females and young males are mainly brown but nonetheless distinctive, with a black crown patch, heavily mottled back and scalloped underparts: the bill and iris are dark brown. The Regent Bowerbird feeds mainly on native fruits but may enter orchards and gardens for cultivated species. The voice, which is seldom heard, includes harsh or chattering notes and some mimicry. It occurs largely in rainforest and neighbouring habitats, where the male constructs a bower of parallel stick walls.

G. Threlfo

Spotted Bowerbird *Chlamydera maculata* 25-31cm

M. Seyfort

Although boldly marked with dark buff spots on the upperparts, this bowerbird is not colourful, except for the iridescent pink nape crest, which may not be visible unless the bird is in display. Sexes are similar but females may lack the crest. The **Western Bowerbird** is darker and more richly coloured. The **Great Bowerbird** is larger, greyer and fairly uniform, lacking the prominent spots. The bower of the Spotted Bowerbird is a platform with two parallel walls of sticks, adorned with bones and snail shells. The voice includes harsh notes and mimicry. It occurs in a range of dry inland woodlands.

131

Great Bowerbird *Chlamydera nuchalis* 34-38cm

M. Seyfort

The male is a dull fawn coloured bird with darker mottling on the upperparts. The magnificent lilac nuchal crest is usually covered and revealed only during courtship display. The sexes are similar but the female often lacks the coloured nape. Using sticks, the male constructs a large avenue bower that is decorated with a variety of objects, including bones and shells. Other species of the genus are smaller and more distinctively marked. The species is found across Australia north of the Tropic of Capricorn, mostly in tropical woodland.

Green Catbird *Ailuroedus crassirostris* 24-33cm

D. Val

The name of this stocky bird refers to its appearance and its voice. The body is bright green above and on the white-tipped wings and tail, paler below, with a pale bill and red iris. Of its various calls, the most easily recognized is a cat-like yowling, frequently heard in rainforests. Although a bowerbird, it does not build a display area. Northwards, it is replaced by the **Spotted Catbird** which has a paler head with black patches on the sides of the face and around the bill; and the **Tooth-billed Bowerbird**, which is brown above and heavily streaked below.

Paradise Riflebird *Ptiloris paradiseus* 25-30cm

Riflebirds are unlike any other Australian bird. Both sexes have long, slender, decurved bills and short tails. The adult male is velvet black above and oily green below; the crown, throat, breast and central tail feathers are iridescent. The female is brown and lacks iridescence but the white eyebrow, reddish wings and arrow-like scalloping on the underparts are distinctive. A loud, explosive 'yas', sometimes given twice, is a characteristic sound in this bird's rainforest habitat. In flight, the male's wings sound like rustling silk. **Victoria's Riflebird**, which replaces it in the north-east, is similar.

L.F. Schick

White-winged Chough *Corcorax melanorhamphos* 43-47cm

R. Brown

The Chough is extremely sociable, almost always seen in groups of up to ten. The curved beak and red iris are unlike any other all black birds. Not visible at rest, the large white wing patch is obvious in flight. The Chough feeds primarily on the ground, moving in groups and raking through the litter. Its presence is often first detected by a mournful, descending whistle. If disturbed, it gives a ratchet-like call. The nest is a large bowl of mud. Members of a group cooperate in caring for their young. Primarily a bird of open forests and woodlands, it also enters modified habitats if not disturbed.

Apostlebird *Struthidea cinerea* 29-33cm

T. & P. Gardner

It is smaller than the **White-winged Chough**, and quite different in appearance but the two species are similar in habits. The Apostlebird has a grey body, dusky brown wings, a black tail and a short stout bill. It travels in troops of 10, occasionally up to 20, individuals, feeding on the ground, searching for food among leaf litter. The nest is a mud bowl, smaller than that of the Chough. The voice is characteristic: a variety of harsh, grating notes, usually uttered when a bird is disturbed. It also occurs in drier forests, woodlands and sometimes near human habitation.

Magpie-lark *Grallina cyanoleuca* 26-30cm

M. Seyfort

Like the **Apostlebird** and **White-winged Chough**, this species builds a mud nest but has little in common with these birds otherwise. Boldly marked black and white, it can be confused with few other birds. The thin whitish bill and pale iris are unlike other similarly coloured species. Adult males have black foreheads and throats; in females these are white; in juveniles, black and white respectively. The 'pee-o-wit' or 'pee-wee' call is frequently given as a duet, each bird raising its wings in turn. Magpie-larks may be found in almost any habitat except rainforest and the driest deserts. They are familiar urban birds.

White-breasted Woodswallow *Artamus leucorynchus* 17-18cm

C. Webster

With its boldly contrasting plumage, this is one of the most easily identified of the woodswallows. A large white rump patch interrupts the dark grey upper wings, tail and upperparts, which are sharply demarcated from the white underparts. This is the only species of Australian woodswallow with no white in the tail, a useful character when viewed from below. The **Masked Woodswallow** has a distinct mask (males black, females grey), a dark rump and white in the tail. From perches and in flight, White-breasted Woodswallows utter their 'pert pert' notes. They are usually found near water, from inland lakes and rivers to coastal mangroves.

Dusky Woodswallow *Artamus cyanopterus* 17-18cm

M. Seyfort

Woodswallows are attractive, sociable birds, often forming mixed flocks of several species. The white wing-stripe separates the Dusky Woodswallow from all others, particularly in combination with its brown body, dark blue-grey wings and white tail tip. The **Little Woodswallow** of northern Australia is smaller, much darker brown and lacks the white wing-stripe. When perched, Dusky Woodswallows have a peculiar habit of wagging their tails side to side. One call has been rendered as a pleasant 'vut vut'. Inhabitants of forests and woodlands, they catch flying insects with graceful swoops from a branch, returning to eat their prey.

White-browed Woodswallow *Artamus superciliosus* 19-21cm

G. Little

This is the most colourful of the woodswallows. The male is dark grey above, with a chestnut breast and belly and a conspicuous white eyebrow. In the female, the underparts are paler and the eyebrow smaller. The **Black-faced Woodswallow** is mainly dusky grey except for a small black facial patch. When overhead, the White-browed Woodswallow frequently gives a musical 'chep chep'. It is highly nomadic and can appear in large numbers after rains in a range of timbered habitats, particularly drier inland woodlands. Like other woodswallows, it feeds mainly on insects, but readily takes nectar when available.

Grey Butcherbird *Cracticus torquatus* 24-30cm

G. Weber

Somewhat incongruously, butcherbirds are excellent songsters but fearsome predators on small animals. The latter practice is indicated by the large, hooked grey and black bill. The adult Grey Butcherbird is attractively plumaged, with a black crown and face, grey back and white throat, underparts and partial collar. Younger birds are largely olive-brown. Its song, a lovely rich piping, makes it welcome around houses, while its predation on small birds has the opposite effect. This species may occur in a variety of wooded habitats, as well as suburban areas. In rainforests and mangroves of the north lives the all-black **Black Butcherbird**.

Pied Butcherbird *Cracticus nigrogularis* 33-37.5cm

L.F. Schick

Larger and more boldly marked than the **Grey Butcherbird**, this species shares that bird's predatory habits and vocal abilities. It is best distinguished from other black and white birds by its black head and upper breast, separated from the black back by a complete white collar, and its large white wing-stripe and robust bill. In flight, the black tail with white corners is conspicuous. Possibly the best singer of all Australian birds, its voice is a beautiful, melodious fluting, sometimes given in alternation by several individuals. It inhabits drier forests and woodlands and will often approach parks and houses.

Australian Magpie *Gymnorhina tibicen* 36-44cm

C. Andrew Henley

The plumage of this large black and white bird varies across its range. Throughout, its nape, upper tail and shoulders are white. Across most of Australia, the remainder of the body is black. In the south-east, centre, extreme south-west and Tasmania, the back and rump are entirely white. The song is a loud musical caroling, often given as duets or by groups. The Magpie is often quite tame but can be aggressive when nesting. It is a common and conspicuous bird usually found where there is a combination of trees and adjacent open areas, including parks and playing fields.

Pied Currawong *Strepera graculina* 44-51cm

G. Little

One of several large black and white birds, this common species is recognized by the white base and tip of the tail, a white patch in the wing, a black bill and yellow iris. The **Grey Currawong** exhibits considerable geographical variation in the amount of white in the wing but none have white at the base of the tail. The name comes from the 'currawong' call. Other frequent vocalisations of the Pied Currawong include guttural croaks and a wolf whistle. A bird of forests and woodlands, it has become well adapted to suburban areas. Large flocks form in winter.

Ravens and Crows *Corvidae* 48-54cm

C. Andrew Henley

Although all are black, the five species of ravens and crows can be separated on a combination of characters. Ravens have grey bases to the neck feathers and crows, white. When calling, the **Australian Raven** raises its long throat hackles and holds its body and head in a horizontal position; the wings are not flicked. The territorial call is a slow 'ah-ah-ah-aaaah' with the last note drawn out. It usually occurs in pairs.

The **Little Raven** has medium length hackles, which are not extended during calling, and the wings are flicked with each note. This species is quite sociable, sometimes forming large flocks. Its call is a much quicker 'kar-kar-kar'. The **Forest Raven** has a proportionally large bill and short tail, and utters a deep 'kor-kor-kor-kor', drawing the last note out. Both crows have more nasal voices and shorter hackles than ravens, and form large flocks. The call of the **Torresian Crow** is 'uk-uk-uk-uk'. Although not flicking its wings when calling, it repeatedly shuffles them after landing. The hackles are raised when calling. The **Little Crow** has a bill shorter than the head and gives a 'nark-nark-nark' call; it does not flick its wings.

Glossary

Adult. A bird that has attained its final plumage form (not including breeding variations) and which is capable of breeding.
Arboreol. Tree dwelling.
Casque. A raised, helmet-like, structure on the head or bill.
Cere. An area of bare skin surrounding the nostrils, at the base of the upper mandible.
Coverts. Feathers that overlap and cover the bases of larger feathers.
Crepuscular. Active in the twilight.
Crest. Long feathers attached to part of the head.
Culmen. The ridge along the length of the upper mandible.
Diagnostic. Individual characteristic used as an aid to identification.
Endemic. Native to the region under consideration.
Eyebrow. A horizontal line above the eye.
Eye-ring. A circle of naked skin or feathers surrounding the eye.
Eye-stripe. A horizontal line that passes from the bill through the eye.
Facial disc. A well-defined and flat area of the face, as in owls.
Family. A category into which an order is divided.
Flush. The act of disturbing a bird and encouraging its flight.
Frontal shield. An unfeathered, horny or fleshy forehead, continued from the base of the upper mandible.
Gape. The unfeathered fleshy area at each corner of the beak.
Genus. A category into which a family is divided.
Hackles. Long throat feathers.
Immature. A bird in the plumage that follows the first moult. Not yet capable of breeding.
Juvenal. A bird in its earliest full-feathered plumage.
Lores. A patch of feathers, often coloured, between base of bill and eye.
Mandible. The upper or lower half of the bill.
Migrant/Migratory. Undertaking regular geographical movement, e.g. from wintering grounds to breeding grounds.
Morph. An alternative plumage colouration possessed by some members of a species.
Nail. A hooked tip of the upper mandible (as in albatrosses, petrels and waterfowl).
Nape. The back of a bird's neck.
Nomadic. Of erratic and changeable movements.
Nuchal Crest. The crest of feathers at the base of the nape.
Nuptial. Pertaining to breeding condition.
Order. One of the major groups into which birds are classified.
Parasitism. The laying of an egg in the nest of another species, which incubates and rears the parasitic young.
Plumage. The layer of feathers or down on the body.
Plume. Long feather used for display.
Primaries. Outer flight feathers.
Rictal bristles. Hair-like structures surrounding the base of the bill.
Roost. A perching place for observation, resting or sleeping.
Secondaries. Inner flight feathers.
Sedentary. Spending the entire life in a relatively restricted region.
Shaft. The main stem of a feather.
Species. The category into which a genus is divided.
Tear-stripe. A vertical marking below the eye.
Territory. An area defended by an individual bird and its family.
Vent. The area from the belly to the undertail coverts.

Further reading

Blakers, M., Davies, S.J.J.F. & Reilly, P.N. (1984) *The Atlas of Australian Birds* Royal Australasian Ornithologists Union, Melbourne University Press, Carlton, Victoria.

Boles, W.E. (1988) *The Robins and Flycatchers of Australia* HarperCollins, Sydney.

Bransbury, J. (1992) *Where to Find Birds in Australia* Waymark Publishing, Fullerton, South Australia.

Cayley, N.W. (1984) (Revised by T.R. Lindsey) *What Bird is That?* HarperCollins, Sydney.

Crome, F. & Shields, J. (1992) *Parrots and Pigeons of Australia* HarperCollins, Sydney.

Forshaw, J.M. and Cooper, W.T. (1984) *Australian Parrots* (Third edition) Lansdowne, Sydney.

Garnet, S. (Ed) (1992). *Threatened and Extinct Birds of Australia* Royal Australasian Ornithologists Union and Australian National Parks and Wildlife Service. RAOU Report 82.

Lindsey, T.R. (1986) *The Seabirds of Australia* HarperCollins, Sydney.

Longmore, W. (1987) *Honeyeaters and their Allies of Australia* HarperCollins, Sydney.

Olsen, P, Crome, F. & Olsen, J. (1993) *Birds of Prey and Ground Birds of Australia* HarperCollins, Sydney.

Pizzey, G. (1991) *Field Guide to the Birds of Australia* (Second edition) A & R Bookworld, Sydney.

Pringle, J.D. (1987) *The Shorebirds of Australia* HarperCollins, Sydney.

Reader's Digest Complete Book of Australian Birds (1993) (Second edition) Reader's Digest, Sydney.

Roberts, P. (1993) *Birdwatcher's Guide to the Sydney Region* Kangaroo Press, Sydney.

Simpson, K. and Day, N. (1993) *Field Guide to the Birds of Australia* Viking O'Neil, Melbourne.

Trounson, A.D. and M. (1994) *Australian Birds Simply Classified* National Book Distributors and Publishers, Sydney.

INDEX (Common Names)

142